Common sense PARENTING

FOURTH EDITION

Using Your Head as Well as Your Heart
to Raise School-Aged Children

$16

1137722

Also from the Boys Town Press

La Crianza Práctica de los Niños Pequeños

Help! There's a Toddler in the House!

Common Sense Parenting®

Common Sense Parenting® DVD Series

    Building Relationships

    Teaching Children Self-Control

    Preventing Problem Behavior

    Correcting Misbehavior

    Teaching Kids to Make Good Decisions

    Helping Kids Succeed in School

Show Me Your Mad Face

Great Days Ahead: Parenting Children Who Have
    ADHD with Hope and Confidence

Raising Children without Losing Your Voice or Your Mind (DVD)

Adolescence and Other Temporary Mental Disorders (DVD)

No Room for Bullies

Good Night, Sweet Dreams, I Love You:
    Now Get into Bed and Go to Sleep

Competing with Character

Practical Tools for Foster Parents

La Crianza Práctica de los Hijos

For Children

For students in Grades K-6, see the back of this book for a list of popular children's titles that highlight important social skills.

For a Boys Town Press catalog, call **1-800-282-6657**
or visit our website: **BoysTownPress.org**

Common sense FOURTH EDITION PARENTING®

Using Your Head as Well as Your Heart to Raise School-Aged Children

RAY BURKE, PH.D. ■ RON HERRON
AND BRIDGET A. BARNES, M.S

BOYS TOWN Press®

Boys Town, Nebraska

Common Sense Parenting®
Published by The Boys Town Press
Father Flanagan's Boys' Home
Boys Town, NE 68010

Copyright © 2015 by Father Flanagan's Boys' Home
ISBN-13: 978-1-934490-81-5

Boys Town Press is the publishing division of Boys Town, a national organization serving children and families.

Publisher's Cataloging-in-Publication

Burke, Raymond V.

Common sense parenting : using your head as well as your heart to raise school-aged children / by Ray Burke, Ron Herron, and Bridget A. Barnes. -- Fourth edition. -- Boys Town, NE : Boys Town Press, [2015]

pages ; cm.

ISBN: 978-1-934490-81-5
Includes index.
Summary: This fourth edition includes new examples of how to approach discipline as positive teaching rather than punishment. Updated parenting techniques are explained step-by-step, with clear examples and action plans for implementing them at home.--Publisher.

1. Child rearing. 2. Parenting. 3. Parent and child. 4. Discipline of children. 5. Parents--Life skills guides. I. Herron, Ronald W. II. Barnes, Bridget A. III. Title.

HQ769

10 9 8 7 6 5 4 3 2 1

Table of Contents

BOYS TOWN NATIONAL HOTLINE®

1-800-448-3000

A crisis, resource and referral number for kids and parents

Introduction

Being a parent is one of the richest and most satisfying experiences you will ever know. Nothing we do as humans is more important than nurturing and teaching a child from infancy to adulthood, preparing him or her not only for what tomorrow holds but also for what life will bring many years from now.

Your children are the most precious gifts you will ever receive. And being a parent is one of the most awesome responsibilities you can take on. Your kids depend on you for love, for guidance, for wisdom, for knowledge — for everything. They look to you for approval, praise, attention, discipline, and affection, no matter how young or old they are.

Of course, some parts of parenting aren't so much fun: the times when you have to wipe runny noses, roust grouchy kids out of bed to get ready for school, taxi them here and there, listen to griping about unfairness and yucky vegetables, or deal with arguing, complaining, and nasty moods. We advise parents to make the best of the good times, learn from and improve on the bad times, and never forget that parenting is a lifelong journey of many steps. What really matters are the bonds you create, the relationships and values that define your family, and what you pass on to your children that can be carried on for generations to come.

All parents can use some help and advice when they are having a tough time with their kids. All parents occasionally doubt their effectiveness. Parenting isn't always easy; we know that. That's why we wrote this book. We work at Boys Town, a national youth care organization that has served as home to tens of thousands of troubled or abandoned children since our founding 1917. What Boys Town has learned about children, parents, and family life has been distilled into our Common Sense Parenting® program and shared with parent trainers and thousands of parents across the United States and in many other countries since 1989.

Through our work, we've heard many parents' stories and shared their triumphs and sorrows. In turn, we've provided our experience and knowledge and shown them a new, positive approach to rearing children. In this book, we hope to share this same knowledge with you and many other parents.

What Common Sense Parenting Can Do for You

What makes Common Sense Parenting work? We emphasize two things: the "head" and the "heart." The "head" means using a logical, practical method of teaching your children; in other words, using teaching and skills to change your kids' behavior. The "heart" means having unconditional love for your children, even in situations where you and your child might be frustrated or upset. Both components are necessary for success. So in addition to teaching you skills to improve your child's behavior, we show you how to work on improving your relationship with your child as well. Put both together and you have a powerful combination.

This book offers you a blueprint for parenting that has been effective with families just like yours. So whether you are a parent who just wants to "brush up" on your parenting skills, an excited "rookie" with your first child, or an exasperated parent with rebellious or difficult children, this book can help you.

We all know that there is no such thing as a perfect parent or a perfect child. We live in a messy, imperfect world and we're going to make mistakes, no matter how hard we try. It's also true that no book, class, or training program alone can solve all of a family's problems. It would be foolish to make such a guarantee. Our lives are too complex to have exact answers for everything. However, the skills you learn in Common Sense Parenting — the logical techniques and foundations for discipline and building relationships — give you a plan for making fewer mistakes and doing a better job in the future. Research studies on the skills and methods we teach show very positive results. Parents who have adopted our approach report that they feel better prepared and more satisfied and effective in their roles as parents, and that their children have fewer behavior problems.

You are your children's first and most important teacher. No one should have a greater impact on your kids' lives than you. That means you have to bring to the task all the love, patience, and energy you can muster. Through all of this, you will find that parenting is the most exciting challenge you will ever face. Make the most of it.

All of the skills in this book rely on one crucial element of parenting. That element is spending time with your kids.

You can teach them only if you are with them. It's as simple as that. You can enjoy the richness of family only if you spend time together. It's absolutely, positively a must. It is the glue that holds a family together.

You are on an exciting path toward becoming a better parent. Your love and the skills you learn in Common Sense Parenting are going to make a positive difference in your family. Love your children even when they least deserve it. Then, teach them the proper way to behave and the skills they need to succeed. Make the most of the opportunities you have with your children, and teach them well.

Using This Book

This revised edition of Common Sense Parenting has five major sections. In the first section, you will learn how to be an effective teacher for your child by learning skills like setting reasonable expectations, using consequences, and giving reasons. In Section II, we show you three techniques that will encourage good behavior and prevent problem behavior by your child. Section III gets to the heart of many parents' frustration and heartache with their children — misbehavior, anger, and defiance. In these chapters, you will learn how to stop and correct misbehavior and teach your child self-control. We also suggest ways for you to stay calm in highly charged confrontations with your child. Chapters in Section IV show you how to put your new parenting skills together by holding Family Meetings, establishing family routines and traditions, and developing your own unique parenting plan. Finally, Section V addresses several special issues that typically create distress in families, including problems at school, peer pressure, and the often negative impact of media and social media (TV, the Internet, etc.).

This book also contains many new reader-friendly features for busy parents. There are reviews that highlight each chapter's main points, key terms and their definitions, many examples that show how parenting skills look and sound so that you can learn how to use them in your family, answers to questions parents commonly ask, and a suggested action plan at the end of most chapters that will help you implement the skills with your children.

We realize that there are no "perfect" answers to the problems that parents face. Each situation, each parent, and each child is unique. For that reason, we offer you practical guidelines and suggestions that can be adapted to your own family and your own "style" of interacting with your children. Applied with your common sense and logic to fit the age and developmental level of your children, our techniques can be used with school-aged children from ages 6 to 16. We hope you use and work on these parenting skills until they become second nature to you. If you use these skills consistently, you can expect to see positive behavior changes in your children.

Change takes time and patience. Learning new behaviors won't occur overnight for you or your child. Things often get worse before they get better. It's much like trying to help your child get over a cold. It takes a while before your chicken soup, Vitamin C, and loving care help your child feel better. So give yourself the necessary time it will take to learn and master these new parenting skills. Expect some difficult times and setbacks, but keep your focus on success. Understand that something as important as improving how you parent your child takes time, effort, and a lot of patience. Learn to look at each improvement as a step in the right direction. Pat yourself on the back when you conquer a problem with one of your kids or when a new parenting skill you're working on starts to make a positive difference in your family's life. The moments of self-doubt you experience will eventually be replaced with renewed confidence in your parenting abilities and ever-increasing enjoyment of the life you and your children share.

Now let's get started!

SECTION I

PARENTS ARE TEACHERS

Anytime you are with your children, you are teaching. Whether you are planning to teach your children or not, teaching is going on all the time. You could be showing your child how to make the bed, correcting him for hitting a sibling, reminding your 6-year-old to put on her coat before running outside, throwing the football with your teenager before the big game, reading a story at bedtime, showing your daughter how to prepare a traditional family dish, helping with homework, or discussing a movie. Regardless of the situation, your words and actions are influencing your kids, your relationship with them, and what they are learning about the difference between right and wrong, and good and bad behavior.

Oftentimes, parents tell us they wish they were better prepared to help their kids learn what they need to know. Wouldn't it be nice to have a plan for parenting, especially when it comes to teaching your kids? Common Sense Parenting offers a plan that not only provides the hows and whys of parenting and being a good teacher, but also allows parents to incorporate their personality and their family's lifestyle into their teaching.

Our plan has three important elements as its foundation:

- **Consistency** – This means parents (or other caregivers) use the same teaching approach, share the same tolerances, and are in agreement when it comes to disciplining their children.

- **Commitment** – This means deciding on and following through with a certain style of teaching, where effective skills provide a step-by-step guide or blueprint for approaching children and their behaviors.

- **Courage** – This means not wavering and staying true to the parenting style you've decided on, even in tough, stressful situations or when children aren't responding as quickly as you'd like or as you'd expect. (Even when you do your best, kids sometimes get worse before they get better.)

In this section, we will introduce the concepts of teaching as a way of disciplining children and how giving children clear messages and expectations makes effective teaching possible. We also will explain reasons and consequences – both positive and negative – and the critical roles they play in bringing about lasting changes in children's behavior. Consequences are essential teaching tools that help children achieve lifelong learning; their influence continues long after the situation in which they've been used ends.

Chapter 1
Discipline Through Positive Teaching

iscipline is often misunderstood and is usually thought of only as something negative. Many parents dread the times when they have to "discipline" their child because it more than likely means tears, tantrums, or stony silence. Some parents get so frustrated and angry over their children's misbehavior that they react violently – either verbally or physically. For these parents, the goal of discipline is to "punish" children for misbehaving. In the short term, punishment may seem to work. In other words, it may stop the child's problem behavior at that moment. But in the long run, slapping, hitting, ridiculing, belittling, isolating, or screaming at children results in all sorts of problems for families, the worst being the damage it does to the relationship between parent and child. In addition, children learn nothing from inappropriate punishment, other than to fear and avoid the parent or to behave violently themselves when they are angry or frustrated.

There are other, much more effective ways to discipline children. We hope to show you in this chapter and throughout this book that discipline can actually be positive, especially when you deal with misbehavior as an opportunity to teach your child. But first, let's look at how you currently might be disciplining your children.

What Kind of Disciplinarian Are You?

Take a moment to review and evaluate your discipline style. Read through the following descriptions of discipline responses. Then choose the five responses that most closely describe the way you react when your children misbehave or you are trying to prevent negative behavior. Rank your five picks, starting with the one you use most frequently. Next to your ranked list, note whether you use those responses seldom, moderately, or frequently. Be honest with yourself so you can get an accurate idea of your discipline style.

When I discipline my child,

1. I use **instructions,** such as, *"You are talking back. Stop talking and listen to me."*

2. I use **negotiation,** such as, *"I'll let you do what you want this time if you promise to...."*

3. I use **explanations,** such as, *"I want you to do this because..."* or *"The reason why you should do what I ask is...."*

4. I use **excuses,** such as, *"It's not really your fault; you've got bad friends"* or *"You should be more responsible but I know it's hard."*

5. I use **negative consequences,** such as, *"Because you didn't do what I asked, you can't watch television tonight."*

6. I use **threats,** such as, *"If you do that one more time, I'm going to..."* or *"Don't make me tell you again, or else."*

7. I use **limits,** such as, *"I know this is hard to accept, but no means no."*

8. I use **judgments,** such as, *"You are such a brat!"* or *"Stop being so lazy."*

9. I use **positive motivators,** such as, *"Because you came home from school on time every day this week, you've earned a later curfew on the weekend."*

10. I use **retaliation,** such as, *"You bit your sister. Now she can bite you."*

11. I use **reaction,** such as, *"I'm fed up! Now, you're going to get it."*

12. I use **preparation,** such as, *"Let's practice a few things to help you stay in school when your friends pressure you to skip class."*

The three most common discipline styles of parenting are: **1) indulgent disciplinarian, 2) strict disciplinarian**, and **3) responsive disciplinarian.** Parents who are indulgent disciplinarians tend to be extremely lenient in their expectations and boundaries for children. Strict disciplinarians usually are not willing to be flexible or open to their children's views on the rules or limits. Parents who are responsive disciplinarians are more willing to negotiate with their children on some rules, but are comfortable enforcing reasonable limits.

How did your discipline assessment turn out? What were your top three discipline responses? If your top choices included 2, 4, and 11, you are more of an indulgent disciplinarian. If 6, 8, and 10 were your top choices, you may be more of a strict disciplinarian. If your top responses included 1, 3, 5, 7, 9, and 12, you are more of a responsive disciplinarian. Most parents use a blend of all three approaches, but your top responses will let you know which style you tend to rely on most often.

Generally, parents who use the responsive disciplinarian approach are more likely to create a positive family environment and are more successful at getting their children to follow the rules and argue less about limits. Common Sense Parenting endorses the techniques of responsive discipline. The aim of this book is to teach you how to learn and incorporate those responsive discipline techniques into your parenting style. For example, if you are mostly indulgent (using excuses, negotiation, and reactions), we recommend that you firm up your approach by learning to use more instructions, limits, and consequences. If you are a parent who is very strict (using judgments, retaliations, and threats), we hope you can become more responsive by making consequences more contingent on behavior and explaining your instructions or rules. Finally, even a responsive approach can be weak or ineffective, if, for example, you are using too many instructions and endless explanations. If this is true for you, you can add more written limits, follow through better on consequences, and react immediately when problems occur.

Positive Teaching

We discipline our children so they will learn how to live cooperatively within our families, in the community, and in the larger society. If you begin to think about discipline as a way to teach your children what they need to know, the situations in which you use discipline will seem less like chores and more like opportunities for your child to learn what he or she will need to know to succeed in the future.

In Common Sense Parenting, we use what we call "positive teaching." All of the skills outlined in this book provide the foundation for and enhance this positive, effective approach to discipline and parenting.

Positive teaching is:

- **Caring** – You let your children know you love them and care about what happens to them.

- **Specific** – You let your children know exactly what they do right or wrong.

- **Responsive** – You help your children understand the relationship between what they do and what happens as a result of their actions.

- **Concrete** – You give your children clear examples of how to improve in the future.

- **Effective** – You help your children learn self-discipline (to be in control of their actions and expressions of emotions).

- **Interactive** – You give your children a chance to show what they have learned. You are an active part of the learning process. You and your children work together toward a common goal.

- **Informative** – You become the teacher and the coach as you give information that helps your children learn to solve problems.

Positive teaching helps build self-confidence, teaches kids to get along well with others, and gives them the skills they need to make their own decisions and control their own behavior. It also helps children learn self-discipline.

We call it positive teaching because children are much more likely to learn when they are treated with affection and pleasantness rather than with anger and punishing behavior. Parents who use positive teaching tell their kids what they did right and why they should continue it, and what they did wrong and how to correct it. Having a good relationship with your child provides a positive framework for learning. If you are pleasant, calm, firm, consistent, and able to give clear messages, your teaching will be effective.

Here are two examples of positive teaching:

Sally and her friend walk into the living room and talk about the new girl in school. Sally's mom overhears Sally tell her friend they shouldn't play with the new girl anymore because she doesn't wear name-brand clothes. Her mom asks the girls to sit down and they talk about how clothes shouldn't determine how someone feels about another person. Mom says it is what's inside a person that is important, not what's on the outside. The girls agree to ask the new girl over after school.

Dad tells Vernon he can't go outside to shoot baskets because he has homework to finish. Vernon gets angry, stomps his feet, and complains that his dad is unfair. Dad tells Vernon they need to talk about Vernon's behavior. First, Dad asks Vernon to calm down and stop yelling. When Vernon is calm,

Dad explains to him he needs to learn to accept "No" for an answer, why it is important to do so, and the appropriate way to do it.

When you learn and practice the techniques of Common Sense Parenting, you'll be able to respond to your children and their misbehavior like these parents did – calmly, lovingly, and with the goal of helping children improve their behavior and become better people.

TIME with Your Children

We've already pointed out that in order to be an effective parent, you must spend time with your children. Here's another way to look at how you spend time with them.

T = **Talk** with your children.

I = **Instruct** your children.

M = **Monitor** your children.

E = **Encourage** your children.

Talking with your children includes clearly describing their behavior so they know what they've done right and what they need to change. Parents also need to discuss why some behavior is acceptable and why other behavior is inappropriate. In other words, give children reasons for why you want them to behave in certain ways. Instruct or teach your children social skills so they learn how to get along with you and others. Teaching and practicing appropriate behavior when children are facing new situations or situations that have given them trouble in the past helps prevent problem behavior. Monitor your children's behavior so you can correct them and give them negative consequences when they make mistakes, or reward them for behavior you want them to repeat. Finally, encourage children by praising what they do well, and build loving relationships by establishing family communication, meetings, routines, and traditions. In the following chapters, we'll look in greater detail at all the individual components of the **TIME** you spend with children.

Summary

Discipline and positive teaching go hand in hand when it comes to good parenting. When parents discipline their children by using teaching that is positive, caring, and specific, they not only address problem behaviors but also build healthier relationships. Teaching is the key to helping children understand right from wrong and to helping them learn positive skills they will use all their lives.

No matter what is happening between parents and their children, parents are always teaching. Children are like sponges, soaking up their parents' words and actions, even when parents think they aren't being heard or watched. When parents take a positive approach to teaching and discipline, they make the most of their opportunities to use their experience and love to shape their children's lives.

✍ CHAPTER REVIEW

What is discipline?

Discipline is the positive teaching and guidance you give children every day to help them understand right from wrong and learn positive social skills.

What does the acronym TIME stand for?

> **T** = **Talk** with your children.
>
> **I** = **Instruct** your children.
>
> **M** = **Monitor** your children.
>
> **E** = **Encourage** your children.

How can positive teaching help children to be self-disciplined?

Positive teaching helps build self-confidence, teaches kids to get along well with others, and gives them the skills they need to make their own decisions and control their own behavior.

☆ ACTION PLAN

1. Take some time to answer the following questions:
   - What is the most important thing you learned in this chapter?
   - What do you plan to do differently as a result of what you've learned?

2. As part of your Action Plan, spend some time this week doing something fun with your child. Let your child take the lead in planning the activity, but tell him or her it shouldn't cost any money and/or it should be something you both enjoy doing.

Q&A
FOR PARENTS

Q I'm a single working parent. How can I do all this teaching? I hardly have time to think.

A There's no question parenting can be difficult when you have little or no support. Even though teaching initially takes some time, it pays off in the long run as your child learns more about and begins using appropriate behavior. Look at it this way: Would you rather spend a few minutes telling and showing your child what your expectations are for his behavior or dealing with a tantrum, tears, or other out-of-control behavior when your child doesn't get his way? Over time, teaching should become second nature to you, and as your child's behavior improves, it should take less and less time.

Q What if I use positive teaching but my child's behavior just gets worse?

A If you feel you need more help, call a professional to assist you. We all need guidance from others at times, especially with some parenting issues. If you don't know how to find a professional, call your child's school or pediatrician, or contact your church. In addition, you can always call the toll-free Boys Town National Hotline® for assistance (1-800-448-3000), anytime day or night.

Will the skills in this book help me parent my special-needs child?

They certainly won't hurt and can only help you. We understand children with special needs may require specific kinds of treatment and support, medically and/or psychologically. If this is the case, parents should seek out professional guidance. However, you can still utilize the skills learned in this book for "everyday" or "routine" concerns regarding your child's behavior.

Chapter 2
Setting Reasonable Expectations

When we ask parents why they are taking our Common Sense Parenting classes, they often answer by telling us they want their children to stop doing some kind of negative behavior. For example, Mom doesn't want her son to argue with her when he's asked to do his chores. Dad says he's tired of his daughter yelling at him when she's told she can't do something. Another parent complains about a son spending hours on his cell phone and a daughter constantly texting. As a result, these parents usually communicate to their children what they don't want them to do: "Don't mouth off at me!" or "Don't you dare pick up that phone." When you constantly focus on children's negative behavior, family life will be filled with angry confrontations, nagging, whining, and defiance.

What we want to teach parents instead, is how to set expectations for children in a reasonable and positive, rather than negative, way. Then, for example, instead of you having to get your kids off the computer or limit their texting each night, they know you expect them to finish their homework before they can play video games for an hour or call or text their friends. Or your daughter knows you expect her to remain calm and say "Okay" if you tell her "No," and your son knows chores must be completed on time before he earns certain privileges each week. This chapter discusses how you can develop reasonable expectations that clearly tell your children how you **do** want them to behave.

Kinds of Expectations

Parents must first decide what kinds of expectations to set for their children. Here is a list of areas where most families have rules or expectations children must meet.

- **Social** — Getting along with others, using greeting and conversation skills, interacting appropriately with the opposite gender, offering to help others, using good manners, saying "Please" and "Thank You."

- **Academic** — Having good study habits and behavior, attending school regularly, completing homework, respecting teachers and administrators, following school rules.

- **Family chores** — Cleaning the bedroom, helping at mealtime, picking up after yourself, helping with outside chores, helping clean the house.

- **Personal appearance and hygiene** — Taking regular showers or baths, wearing clean and appropriate clothing, putting away personal items, using soap and deodorant.

- **Religious** — Attending services with the family, praying, volunteering for activities, living up to the family's religious standards.

The first step in developing clear expectations is to identify those that are already in place in your family. On a sheet of paper, list some of the expectations in these five areas you already have for your kids. Then add any you think are needed to address problems you are having with your children's behavior in these areas.

Expectations Must Be Reasonable

Now that you have some examples of your own to work with, let's take a look at whether those expectations are reasonable for your children. To do this, you must consider whether expectations are appropriate for your kids' ages, abilities, and resources. We won't go into a long description about developmental milestones for children; there are many good books that explain stages of child development. But from a practical standpoint, common sense can often tell us what we can expect from kids at certain ages. For example, it would be reasonable to expect that an average 6-year-old can learn how to set the dinner table. It would require teaching and assistance from you, but it is a reasonable expectation. However, it would be unreasonable to think the same 6-year-old could prepare the meal. Even with your best teaching, it is highly unlikely a 6-year-old could follow a recipe, measure ingredients accurately, and safely cook the meal on the stove. Expecting a 6-year-old to prepare a meal would be an unreasonable expectation because it would be inappropriate for his or her age, abilities, and resources.

Other than using common sense, are there other ways to tell whether an expectation is reasonable or not? Ask yourself the following three questions about each expectation you have for your child. If you can answer "Yes" to all three, then you probably have set a reasonable expectation for that child.

23

Have you taught and modeled the expectation to your child?

It is unreasonable to expect children to do something if you haven't specifically taught it to them or demonstrated it through your own behavior. Later chapters in this book will show you how to teach your children the various skills they will need to be successful. In particular, we'll show you how to use Preventive Teaching (Chapter 7) to teach your child the behaviors you want to see from him or her.

Can your child understand the expectation?

One way to check for understanding is to have your child describe the expected behavior to you in his or her own words. For example, can your child tell you what needs to be done in order to make his bed? Your child may not use the exact words you use, but the description will indicate whether your expectations are clear and whether he understands them.

Can your child demonstrate what you expect?

Ask your child to show you what you have taught. If the child can demonstrate the task reasonably well, then your expectation is probably within the child's abilities.

Clarifying Expectations

Now that you've made sure your expectations are reasonable, you need to make sure they are clear to your children. You can do this, first by stating expectations in a positive way **(what you say)**, and second, by following through, in a consistent way, on your children's efforts to meet your expectations **(what you do)**.

What you say. Expectations are usually clearer and more effective when you describe them in a positive way, instead of telling your kids what not to do. Use "do" instead of "don't" statements, or follow a "don't" statement immediately with a "do" statement. For example, when you tell your 10-year-old, "Don't drop your schoolbooks in the hallway," follow it with, "Please take them to the desk in your bedroom." By positively describing your expectations, you make it clear what your child should do now and in the future. Several other examples of how to replace "don't" with "do" expectations are listed here.

Don't: *"When I ask you to help clean the kitchen, don't talk back and roll your eyes."*

Do: *"When I ask you to help clean the kitchen, say 'Okay' and start the job right away."*

Don't: *"I don't want you grabbing things from your sister."*

Do: *"Ask your sister to share when she has something you want. If she says 'Yes,' wait until she's finished. If she says 'No,' find another toy."*

Don't: *"Don't yell and complain when I tell you that you can't do something."*

Do: *"When you ask me to do something and I tell you 'No,' just say 'Okay.' If you don't understand, calmly ask me to explain it to you."*

Don't: *"Don't sneak off and use your phone when you're supposed to be doing your homework."*

Do: *"Start your homework right away when you get home from school. You can text your friends when you're finished."*

What you do. If your children do what's expected of them, let them know by praising the behavior that is consistent with your expectations. If you expect them to do their homework right after school and you find them doing it, make sure you follow through by giving them any privileges they've earned. If you tell your kids "No" after they've asked to go to a friend's house, and they accept your answer by saying "Okay," praise them for accepting your answer.

You also need to correct behavior that does not match your expectations. If your children argue with you after you tell them "No," follow through with a consequence. (We'll discuss giving consequences in Chapter 4.) Again, be consistent. Letting them argue and whine after you tell them "No" on some occasions and correcting them on others is confusing to children.

Clarity comes both from what you say and what you do in response to your children's behavior. Your behavior should also be consistent with your expectations for your children. If you want your kids to disagree calmly, give them a good example to follow by staying calm when you have a disagreement with them. If you expect your children to attend church weekly, attend with them. If you want your kids to read more and do better in school, turn the TV off and read with them. Many times, actions really do speak louder than words. Be a consistent and positive role model. Your children will have a much clearer understanding of your expectations when you do.

Examples of Expectations

The following are two lists of reasonable expectations for children according to their age. In many families, expectations are understood but unwritten. In other families, parents and children have discussed expectations and have written them down. If you write down your expectations, don't overwhelm children by making the list too long. Focus the list on your most important expectations; you can simply discuss other expectations so everyone in the family understands them. However you choose to convey your expectations to your children, all family members should be aware of them. You can discuss them individually by using Preventive Teaching (covered later in Chapter 7) or you can discuss them as a group at Family Meetings (covered later in Chapter 14).

Expectations for Younger Children

1. Keep your feet off the furniture so you don't lose any of your play time.

2. When you come home, hang your coat where it belongs and put your shoes in your closet. Then, you may have a snack.

3. When everyone is finished eating, clean your plate and put it in the sink before having dessert.

4. Volunteer to either help set the table or help clean up after dinner in order to earn TV time.

5. Bedtime is at 8:30 and we start getting ready at 7:30. If you are ready for bed by 8 p.m., we'll have time to read a story.

6. Say your prayers before each meal and before going to bed.

7. Ask permission before you turn on the TV.

8. Flush the toilet and wash your hands after you go to the bathroom.

9. Never talk to strangers (including on the telephone or computer) or never let anyone into the house unless you check with Mom or Dad.

10. Get your books and school supplies ready before you go to bed each night so you have time for breakfast in the morning.

Expectations for Older Children

1. When you complete your homework and have it checked, you may watch TV, use the phone, or play on the computer.

2. When you study or read for at least one hour on Sunday through Thursday nights, you earn time to go out with friends on Friday or Saturday night.

3. When you want to go out on the weekends, ask at least two days in advance (Wednesday for Friday, Thursday for Saturday). This helps avoid problems with using the car and helps organize the family's schedule.

4. In order to use the car, ask at least one day in advance. Bring it back with the same amount of gas, and be willing to wash it when we think it is necessary.

5. Please limit your phone calls and texting each evening. All calling, texting, and social media ends before 10 p.m.

6. Before asking to go anywhere or to do anything, complete all schoolwork and house- work (make bed, clean room, put clothes where they belong).

7. If you disagree with an answer, disagree calmly without arguing. We will listen to you. When you argue, you lose 15 minutes or more from your curfew.

8. Put your dirty clothes in the laundry basket. If you leave dirty clothes in your room, it will be your responsibility to fold the next load of wash.

9. Attend church once a week with the family. Participate in at least one volunteer activity at church each month. If you don't feel well enough to go to church, you're not well enough to go out with your friends.

10. Before going out, be prepared to answer questions like: Where are you going? What are you going to do? Who will you be with? When do you plan to be back?

One final word about clear expectations: Two-parent families need to have consistent expectations and methods of discipline. For some parents, agreeing on expectations is a problem. One parent may think the other is being unrea- sonable, either too strict or too lax. It takes constant effort for two parents who may have different approaches to parenting to set expectations they can both agree on. Parents must learn to negotiate with one another. It also is important for them to agree not to argue about expectations in front of the

CONSISTENCY AND ROUTINES

Throughout this book, we talk about how important it is for parents to be consistent. Consistency is setting up and following family routines, rules, and expectations children understand and can depend on. Consistency helps kids feel secure and encourages good behavior.

For example, one single mother and her two kids do most of their laundry on Sunday. They spend the evening folding the laundry and watching TV together until 10 p.m., when the kids go to bed. In another family with smaller children, a parent starts getting them ready for bed at 7:30 each evening. First, they turn off the TV, then the kids get into their pajamas and brush their teeth. Those who stayed in bed the night before get an extra bedtime story from Mom or Dad. Finally, they end the routine with nightly prayers and a bedtime song.

Now, routines like these don't work perfectly every night and there are occasional activities, telephone calls, or meetings that interrupt the schedule. But these are the exceptions, not the rule. In general, these kids can expect some time with their parents at the end of the day, and bedtime problems decrease measurably.

Kids need structure. It helps them learn responsible behaviors. They know what they should do and when they should do it. For kids, consistency and daily routines help reduce problems and confusion. For parents, consistent daily routines reduce hassles and make a home run much more smoothly.

$\Longrightarrow$

kids. When parents can't agree, it makes life confusing and problematic for everyone in the family. It's worth the effort for both parents to be consistent with their expectations for their children's behavior. In the long run, setting clear expectations benefits everyone in the family.

Summary

Clear expectations help children understand what they should and shouldn't do, and provide a framework for positive behavior. Even though kids won't meet your expectations all of the time, having clear and reasonable expectations should improve their behavior. When setting expectations, remember to ask yourself three important questions: "Have I taught and modeled what I expect? Does my child understand what I expect? Can my child demonstrate what I expect?" If you can answer "Yes" to all of these questions, you've done a great job of setting clear and reasonable expectations.

ᗯᕦ CHAPTER REVIEW

How do I develop reasonable expectations?

Ask yourself, "What expectations are appropriate for my kids' ages, abilities, and resources?" Once you've determined this, answer the following questions: "Did I teach my child exactly what I expect? Does my child understand the expectations? Can he or she demonstrate these expectations?"

How can I clarify my expectations?

Clarify your expectations through teaching and modeling. Expectations are usually clearer and more effective when you describe and model them in a positive way, instead of telling kids what not to do.

How can I encourage improvements toward expectations?

You must praise positive behavior that meets your expectations and correct negative behavior that does not.

☆ ACTION PLAN

1. Answer the following questions regarding what you learned in this chapter:

    *   What is the most important thing you learned in this chapter?

    *   What do you plan to do differently as a result of what you've learned?

2. Here's an activity that can get the whole family thinking about reasonable expectations.

    *   Gather one paper bag, scissors, and a piece of paper and a pencil for each family member.

    *   Ask everyone to write down what he or she expects from other family members. Help younger children make a list of things they think others should do to support them. (For example, Mom could write, "I expect a hug." Dad could write, "I expect everyone to pitch in with the yard work on the weekends before they go off to play or visit with their friends." A young child could request, "I want my brother to play a video game with me.")

- Cut the lists up so there is one expectation on each slip of paper. Put the slips in the paper bag. (Optional: Tape wrapped pieces of candy to the slips of paper.)
- Write "Grab Bag" on the front of the bag and put it in an accessible location. (Not too accessible for young children if you include the candy!)
- Encourage family members to take a slip of paper out of the bag once a day or once a week and to make an effort to do what's suggested on it for someone else in the home.

Q&A
FOR PARENTS

Q **How many times do I have to demonstrate something for my daughter before I can expect her to do it correctly on her own?**

A It takes a while for children to develop competency and consistency with skills. This is especially true when kids have had difficulty with a skill in the past or if they're learning a new skill. So the answer is: It depends — it depends on her age, her developmental level, her familiarity with the skill. You may need to practice the skill a number of times with her. Be patient and praise her improvements.

Q **What if my husband has one expectation and I have another?**

A It's important that both of you agree on expectations, especially when they involve major issues about your kids and family. Talk about family rules, behaviors, activities, and expectations and how you both plan to handle them. If you disagree on an issue, talk about this privately, away from the children. See if you can reach a compromise you both can live with, and be consistent on it with your children.

Q **I've never had a lot of expectations for my kids. When I do try to set some rules they just laugh at me.**

A Setting expectations in a home where there haven't been any in the past isn't easy, but it can be done! The key is to stay committed and consistent. Also, make sure you back up your expectations with clear teaching, consequences, and encouragement — parenting skills we will talk about in future chapters.

How can I get my child's school to support the expectations I have for him?

Enlist the school's support by talking to your child's teachers about the behavior you are trying to teach him. For example, if you are trying to get your child to follow instructions at home, explain this to his teachers. Thank them in advance for helping you reinforce this behavior. Then, you can send a "school note" with your child and ask his teachers to make a mark on it to indicate each time your child follows or fails to follow instructions at school. At home, you can give positive rewards or negative consequences to your child, depending upon the behaviors reported on the school note.

I have the bad habit of telling my children what I don't want them to do. How can I break myself of being so negative?

First, don't be too hard on yourself. It's very easy for parents to focus on what's wrong with kids. You've taken the first step by admitting you do this. Next, you can set a specific goal for yourself, such as trying to positively describe what you want your children to do once each morning, once after school, and again before bedtime. Track how well you do by adding checkmarks to a card you keep handy. Doing this deliberately for a while should help you focus on giving positive descriptions more naturally and more often in the future.

Q **Sometimes when my children come home from visiting other relatives, their behavior is much worse than at home. Should I stop these visits?**

A No. It's unrealistic to expect the rules and expectations you have for your children to be identical to those of others everywhere they go. Instead, tell your children that when they visit relatives' homes, you expect them to use the skills and practice the good behavior you have taught them, wherever they are. Follow up with positive and negative consequences. When they return home, remind them again of the rules, expectations, and routines that apply in your home.

Chapter 3
Giving Clear Messages

"You've got a lousy attitude!"
"Stop being so naughty."
"I'm proud of how you acted this week."
"Thanks for being so nice at the store today."

As parents, we've all probably made comments like these to our children. But do children always understand exactly what behavior we're talking about when we use words like "lousy," "naughty" or "nice"? Probably not. Most children are concrete thinkers; abstract or vague descriptions can leave them confused or frustrated.

Read those comments again. Do they give you a clear picture of how those children were actually behaving? Instead of saying a child had a "lousy attitude," that parent could have told his child, *"When I asked you to pick up your shoes, you walked away from me and mumbled, 'Get off my back.'"* Or instead of telling her son he was a "nice" boy at the store, that mom could have said, *"You walked quietly beside the cart and helped me find the groceries on our list. That was nice."* With these statements, parents would be giving their children very specific information; these kids would clearly understand which behaviors their parents are either trying to change or to compliment.

Giving clear messages like this is a key to effective positive teaching. As a parent, you must be specific when telling your children what needs to be done and how to do it. You need to clearly let your children know when they've done well so they can repeat that behavior, and also be clear when they've misbehaved so they know what behavior you want them to change. This means focusing on what children are doing or saying, and accurately describing their behaviors.

What Is Behavior?

What happens when you listen to a football game on the radio? Good sports announcers help you visualize what is happening on the field by giving vivid descriptions. They don't just tell you, for example, that your team scored a touchdown. They describe how the quarterback dropped back from the line of scrimmage, scrambled away from a blitzing lineman, and then threw the football 20 yards down the field to a receiver in the end zone. Good announcers help you "see" every play clearly. Parents need to be just as clear with their kids when describing their behavior.

What exactly is behavior? **Behavior is what people do or say. Or, behavior is anything a person does that can be seen, heard, or measured.** Here are some good descriptions of specific child behaviors:

"My daughter talks on the phone for one hour at a time."

"When I ask my son to do something, he rolls his eyes and walks away."

"When my kids come home from school, they put their

books away and ask if there's anything that needs to be done around the house."

"When I tell my daughter her jeans are too tight, she whines and asks me why I'm always on her back."

"My son helps me put away the dishes, then rinses the sink and sweeps the kitchen floor."

When you read these descriptions, you can visualize what these children are doing. It's easy to understand what we mean by a person's actions that can be seen or heard. But parents often ask, "What does it mean to 'measure' behavior?" Here are two examples: Playing video games or helping with the dishes are behaviors — what a person does. You can measure how long your son plays video games by the amount of time he spends at the computer. You can measure how often your daughter helps you with the dishes by putting a check mark on the calendar every time she does it. Measuring how often or how long a behavior occurs is another way of clearly describing behavior.

Giving Clear Messages

In order to give clear messages, you must first watch what your child does or says. Then, clearly and specifically tell your child what was done correctly or incorrectly. This is like giving an instant replay of the behavior. Use words you know your child will understand. For younger children, use short sentences and easily understood words. As they get older, adjust your language to fit their age and level of understanding.

When giving clear messages, it helps to describe some of the following:

Who is involved? Who is being praised? Whose behavior is being corrected?

What just happened? What was done well? What needs to be improved or changed?

When did the behavior happen?

Where did the behavior occur?

How you give messages is also very important. Here are several points that will help you convey clear messages to your children:

- **Try to position yourself so you are at eye level with your child.** Avoid intimidating your child by standing over him or her.

- **Have your child look at you.** This makes it more likely that your child will hear what you say and follow through on any requests. Our experience has taught us eye contact is a key to giving and receiving clear messages.

- **Look at your child.** This allows you to see your child's reaction to what you say. Give your child your full attention. When both of you are looking at each other, it helps improve communication.

- **Use a voice tone that fits the situation.** Your voice should be firm when giving correction, friendly and enthusiastic when giving compliments and praise.

- **Eliminate as many distractions as possible.** Try to find a quiet area where you can talk to your child.

Let's compare vague descriptions of kids' behavior with specific descriptions of the same situation.

Vague   *"Billy, please act your age when our company arrives."*

Specific   *"Billy, when our guests get here, make sure you say 'Hi.' Then you can go to your room and play."*

Vague   *"When we get to the store, please be a nice girl."*

Specific   *"When we get to the store, remember we aren't buying any candy. I'd like you to help me pick out the things on our list and put them in the cart. You can also push the shopping cart. Okay?"*

Vague   *"That was a nice story you wrote for English class, Reggie."*

Specific   *"Reggie, you did a nice job on your story for English class. You used complete sentences and all of the grammar was correct."*

Vague   *"Sam, quit eating like a pig!"*

Specific   *"Sam, you're eating with your fingers and making noises while you eat. Please use your fork, take small bites, and don't make any noise."*

The specific statements are accurate descriptions of what these children said or did or what the parent wanted them to do or say. These clear messages enhance children's understanding and increase the likelihood they will use appropriate behavior in the right situations.

Summary

One final thought about clear messages: An important part of being specific when describing your children's misbehavior is that they understand you dislike their behavior, not them. You may be upset and displeased with the way your child is acting, but you still love your child. That's why you are taking the time to teach him or her another way to behave.

Later in the book you will see how clear messages fit into a framework for praising and correcting your kids. Giving clear messages helps you become a better teacher and helps your children change their behavior. Clear messages are crucial to making all the other teaching techniques work. In the next chapter, we'll add another valuable part of our teaching methods — giving consequences.

☞ Chapter Review

What is behavior?

Behavior is anything a person does that can be seen, heard, or measured.

What are clear messages?

Clear messages specifically and clearly tell your child what behavior he or she has done correctly or incorrectly.

Why is it important for parents to use clear messages?

Children are more likely to understand you and how you want them to behave in certain situations.

☆ ACTION PLAN

1. Take time to answer the following questions:
   - What is the most important thing you learned in this chapter?
   - What do you plan to do differently as a result of what you've learned?

2. Here's an activity that can help your family work on clear communications:
   - You will need a tennis ball and the Grab Bag you made as part of the activity at the end of Chapter 2.
   - During the week, have family members sit down in a circle and have a 10-minute discussion. The discussion should focus on what unexpected acts of kindness family members did for each other that week. Also discuss whether any of the expectations in the Grab Bag were unreasonable.
   - Take turns talking by tossing the ball around to each family member so everyone has a chance to speak. Whoever has the ball gets to talk.
   - Anyone who did not go to the Grab Bag during the previous week should immediately take a slip of paper from the bag and carry out the expectation written on it as soon as possible.

Q&A
FOR PARENTS

Q **If my child is lazy, what's wrong with telling him he is lazy?**

A The word "lazy" is not clear and specific enough. It doesn't tell your child exactly what he is doing wrong or how to change his behavior.

Q **My child already knows how to clean her room. Why should I have to specifically describe how to do it?**

A If she clearly knows what your expectations are for a "clean room" and has successfully met your criteria in the past, then you may not have to describe anything. But for many kids, their idea of what a clean room looks like is a far cry from what their parents expect. Take the guesswork out of it and specifically describe to your child exactly what you expect. This will help prevent any misunderstanding and set your child up for success.

Q **How long will I have to tell my child what I expect before she can figure it out on her own?**

A It depends on your child. Every child is different and learns at a different rate. Some kids pick things up quicker than others, while some need more time to learn. Be patient, teach clearly, and use encouragement. Allow each and every one of your children the time needed to learn and become more self-disciplined.

Q **My parents never did do a lot of talking with me. I just watched them and learned. Why are my kids so different?**

A Your children probably aren't all that different. What is different today may be your family's lifestyle, the number of distractions in the home, the time kids spend away from home and family, and, sometimes, the lack of good parent-child communication. That's why it's important to use clear and specific communication; this can help build stronger bonds between you and your children.

Q **My son uses a lot of slang when he talks to me. He says it's his right to express himself. Should I forbid him from talking that way?**

A Every generation of youngsters uses some sort of slang to express their thoughts and feelings. This doesn't mean they need to use it all the time and with everyone. There is a time and place for "their" language, and it's up to you to teach your children when and where that language is appropriate and not appropriate. For example, you can teach that it's okay to use slang when your kids are playing or talking with their friends, but not appropriate when they are greeting adult visitors to your home.

CHAPTER 4
Using Consequences to Change Behavior

M uch of what we do as human beings is motivated either by something positive we expect to happen as a result of our behavior or a desire to avoid something negative. For example, we work at a job because we get personal satisfaction and/or a paycheck. We strive to be on time for that job to avoid getting negative feedback from the boss or being fired for tardiness. If we do arrive late and receive a written warning, we try harder not to be late again. These positive or negative experiences that flow from our behavior are called **consequences**. Likewise, consequences teach children there are outcomes for the way they act. Children often need motivation to change their behavior. You can use consequences as motivation when you are teaching your children how you want them to behave.

We see consequences as teaching tools parents can use to encourage a child's appropriate behavior or reduce a child's misbehavior. For example, if you give your daughter something she likes (praise or an extra privilege) when she helps clear the dirty dishes after dinner, she is likely to do it again because she likes being rewarded. If you take away something your son likes (use of the car on the weekend) or give him something he doesn't like (an extra chore) for using the car without permission, he is less likely to take the car without asking first.

Consequences can be defined as anything that follows a behavior that may cause that behavior to happen more often or less often in the future. Consequences are not a magical cure-all for children's misbehavior, nor are they guaranteed to automatically increase a child's use of positive behaviors. As important as they are, they are only one component of the bigger picture of effective parenting through teaching. The real value of consequences in parenting usually isn't seen until they have been used correctly and consistently, over a period of time, in the context of a loving relationship between parent and child, and as part of a positive approach to parenting. Although they may not be the answer to all of your concerns about your child's behavior, consequences are a proven way to help bring about changes in that behavior.

Using consequences to address kids' behavior is a must. Consequences remind children to think. They teach children there is a connection between what they do and what happens to them and the people around them. Children learn life is full of choices and the choices they make greatly influence what happens to them and the people around them. When parents give effective consequences, children learn successful ways to behave.

How Consequences Help Change Behavior

Because consequences that are used correctly and consistently can be so influential in helping change behavior, it makes sense that we would use them to teach our kids right from wrong. You've probably used consequences many times before. "Grounding" your child for coming home late, letting your teenager drive the family car for helping around the house, or offering dessert only after children have eaten dinner and helped clear the table — these all are examples of how privileges and chores can be used as consequences.

Let's look at some of the elements of effective consequences. There are two primary kinds of consequences — positive and negative.

Positive consequences are things people like and are willing to work to get. Behavior followed by a positive consequence is more likely to occur again. Rewards, praise, attention, and privileges are forms of positive consequences. They can range from a few words of simple praise or a special snack to a later curfew or more time with friends.

Negative consequences are things people don't like and want to avoid. Behavior that is followed by a negative consequence is less likely to occur again (or will not occur as frequently). Removing a reward or privilege like a trip to the store or a visit to a friend's house, or adding a chore, are negative consequences.

How you use five variables in giving consequences determines how effective your consequences will be. These variables are importance, immediacy, frequency, size, and contingency. When these variables are used correctly, consequences have the desired effect, which is to bring about long-term behavior change.

Importance

The consequence you give has to mean something to your child. Taking away or giving something that doesn't interest your child will not help change behavior. One way to find out what is important to your child is to watch what he or she does during free time. Perhaps your young son likes to watch cartoons, invite friends over, and ride his bicycle. Because these activities are enjoyable to him, they can be used as effective consequences.

Immediacy

Parents should give a consequence right after a behavior occurs. If you can't give the consequence right away, tell the child he or she has earned a consequence and then give it as soon as possible. Do your best not to delay acknowledging the behavior or giving the earned consequence. Delay reduces the impact of the consequence and weakens the connection between the behavior and the consequence. For example, if you take away play time for an argument your 8-year-old daughter got into two days ago, she may have forgotten her misbehavior, be confused about why she has earned a consequence, and think you are being very unfair.

Frequency

How often you give a consequence is important as well. If you give the same consequence too often, it may lose its effectiveness. For example, if you were to give your son time to play on the computer (assuming he likes that) every time he helps around the house, he might work like crazy to earn extra time for a while. Over time, however, he may become less helpful. Why? Because he might reach a saturation point where more time on the computer means little to him, and he will no longer be motivated to work to earn more time. So it's more effective to vary your consequences.

Size

Always try to match the size of the consequence to the importance of the behavior. In other words, give a consequence you think is just large enough to either encourage or discourage the behavior you are targeting. This should work for both positive and negative consequences. So if you think allowing your child to have a friend stay over Saturday night will be incentive enough for her to keep her room clean during the week, use that as the positive consequence. Grounding your daughter for a month for not cleaning her room, however, is a negative consequence that is too large for the problem behavior. A less severe consequence (for example, not allowing her to have a friend stay over during the weekend) would probably get the job done.

Giving large positive consequences for minor behaviors may result in a "spoiled" child — one who gets too much for doing too little. On the other hand, giving large negative consequences for relatively small misbehaviors may make a child feel like he or she is always being punished. If you have a child who is constantly doing inappropriate behavior, you should start off giving the smallest consequence you think will effectively change the behavior. This will help manage the amount of consequences your child accumulates for these high-frequency misbehaviors.

Contingency

This is commonly called **"Grandma's rule"** because wise grandmothers used it long before it ever showed up in a book. This rule mandates that an activity (a privilege your child likes) is available only after your child finishes a specified task. That is, one activity is contingent on the other.

Parents can use this contingency rule with kids of all ages. Here are some examples:

- *"You can watch TV **after** you have finished your homework."*
- *"**Because** you put your dirty clothes in the laundry basket and made your bed, you can go outside."*
- *"**When** you're finished with the dishes, you can call your friend."*

Let's look at an example of how using all five of these variables determines how well a consequence works:

Lisa's father comes downstairs and sees that Lisa has picked up after her friends. In the past, Lisa has left the family room a mess until one of her parents instructed her to clean it. Lisa's father knows she loves to text her friends. So, he finds Lisa in the kitchen and creates a teaching moment by saying, *"The family room looks great! Thanks for remembering to clean up. Because you followed instructions and cleaned the room* (contingency), *you've **earned an extra 15 minutes** (size) on the **phone** (importance) **tonight** (immediacy)."* This is a positive consequence Lisa's parents initially use (frequency) to help reinforce behavior they want to see again. What if Lisa didn't clean up after her friends as her parents asked? Her dad can take away phone time as a negative consequence. For example, he could say, ***"Because you did not follow instructions and clean the family room*** (contingency), *you've **lost your texting privileges on the phone** (importance) **tonight** (immediacy)."*

When Consequences Aren't Working

Parents occasionally tell us that no matter what they try, the consequences they are using aren't working with their kids. In some cases, it is possible their children have problems that are too complicated for them to handle alone. In those situations, we would suggest they see a professional counselor to support their parenting. More often than not, however, there are some basic reasons why consequences are ineffective. The most frequent problems occur when parents use consequences that aren't appropriate in one or more of the five variables we mentioned earlier: importance, immediacy, frequency, size, and contingency. In other words, the consequences they are using may be too big, too small, not important enough to their children, aren't happening soon enough after the target behavior, etc.

However, there are other reasons why consequences don't work. First, parents sometimes give a lot of negative consequences and not many positive consequences. As a result, the negative consequences lose their effectiveness because kids start seeing their parents as punishing. If they are rarely rewarded for good behavior at home, children may stop trying. When parents don't provide a healthy balance between positive and negative consequences, children will start avoiding them and look elsewhere for positive consequences. In these situations, kids find it's just too unpleasant to be around their parents.

Second, some parents don't give consequences enough time to work. They expect a child's behavior to change after using a consequence only once or twice. It usually doesn't work that way; change takes time. Children may have used the negative behaviors over a long period of time. It may take as much time or more for them to learn and consistently use a new, positive behavior. So don't give up if your child's behavior doesn't change overnight or even gets worse before it gets better. Be patient, look for small improvements, and give the consequences time to work.

Finally, some parents confuse privileges with rights. Children are entitled to certain rights, including love, nourishment, clothing, shelter, safety, and so on. (These should never be withheld as consequences for misbehavior.) However, many kids try to convince their parents that things like watching TV, going out with their friends, or having a cell phone, are rights as well. But these are privileges parents can, and should, be able to give or withhold from children depending on their behavior. If parents treat privileges as rights, they limit what they can use for consequences, and therefore limit their effectiveness as teachers. Later in the chapter, we will help you identify privileges you can use as consequences with your children.

Plan Ahead

Some parents have told us that when it comes time to actually give a consequence, they have a hard time coming up with an effective one, or circumstances make it difficult for the child to follow through on it. When this happens, simply tell the child he or she earned a consequence (positive or negative). Then, at a calmer moment, decide on the consequence and give it as soon as possible. Here's how this might work: Mom is on the phone with an important call. Her 8-year-old son, Bobby, interrupts by asking several times if he can have a cookie. This is a behavior Mom is trying to stop, so she asks the caller to hold for a second and says to Bobby, *"Honey, you've earned a consequence for interrupting me while I'm on the phone. When I get off, we'll talk about your consequence."* Also, in situations when you're upset with a child, this gives you time to cool down and avoid blasting him or her with a big consequence: *"You're interrupting me again. Go to your room and stay there for the rest of the day!"*

Being prepared also can involve setting up both positive and negative consequences in advance. You can even make a general list of privileges and chores children can earn or lose as rewards and punishments for behavior. Your consequences will be more effective if you give them naturally (as part of real life) and with confidence, and they are calmly thought out in advance. Being prepared also helps you avoid using consequences as weapons for your emotions *("I've had it with you! Now you're going to get it!")*. Oftentimes, your best teaching (and your child's best learning) will occur when you have taken some time to think about what you want to teach and which consequence to use.

When at all possible, your child should know in advance what consequences you will use for specific behaviors, especially ones you are focusing on. These can include frequent behaviors like arguing with you and rarer, severe ones like hitting a sibling. Talk with your kids about positive consequences they can expect to earn for good behavior and negative consequences they can expect for misbehavior. Post your lists of consequences on the refrigerator door or in your children's rooms as reminders. Consequences shouldn't necessarily be surprises. In fairness to your children, they should be aware of what good things they can earn for behaving well and what they will lose for misbehavior. However, children don't need to know every consequence that might be given. What's important is that they understand consequences will be given consistently for certain behaviors.

In Chapter 8, on charts and contracts, we talk about help-ing your child set and reach reasonable goals. Parents tell us this also is a good way to spell out positive and negative con-sequences for their children. When a negative consequence is involved, children also should know they might have an opportunity to earn back (or reduce) some of the consequence. (The concept of earning back some of a consequence will be discussed in Chapter 10, "Correcting Misbehavior.")

Giving Consequences

How you give consequences is nearly as important as the consequences themselves. Whether your child has earned either a positive or negative consequence, your behavior has a lot to do with whether it will have the desired effect.

Positive consequences should be given with much enthu-siasm and praise. You should make it clear you appreciate your child's good behavior and you want that behavior to continue. Children are more likely to respond well if they receive positive consequences from parents who are pleas-ant, enthusiastic, and sincere. Showing appreciation, combined with the effective positive consequence of giving attention, is a successful formula for motivating children to repeat good behavior.

Negative consequences should be given in a calm, firm voice that lets a child know the situation is serious. They should not be given in anger because that usually results in more problems. Parents who are upset by a child's problem behavior can easily let that carry over to when they give negative consequences. Therefore, you must keep your own emotions under control when you give negative conse-quences. Don't shout, talk fast, point fingers, or call names. In other words, don't let your behavior make the consequence more negative than it already is. After you have given a negative consequence, think about what you said and did and decide if there are things you should change in the future so your teaching can be more effective.

Our experience tells us children respond better and learn more from adults who are encouraging, calm, and empathetic — even when they are giving negative consequences. Although staying calm is crucial to effective teaching, parents tell us it's one of the hardest things for them to do. For that reason, we wrote a chapter that provides suggestions on how to keep your cool during stressful times with your kids. (See Chapter 9, "Staying Calm.")

More information on giving negative consequences as part of correcting misbehavior and dealing with frequent and severe behavior can be found in Chapters 10 and 11.

Helpful Hints

Here are some hints to help you understand how your behavior affects the outcome when you give your child a consequence. When giving a consequence, remember to:

Be clear. Make sure your child knows what he or she did to earn the consequence.

Be consistent. Don't give a big consequence for a behavior one time and then ignore the same behavior the next time.

Be brief. Don't lecture. This is especially true with younger children. Stay focused on the situation and calmly let your children know what they did and what consequence they earned.

Follow through. If you set up a plan for your child to earn a positive consequence, be sure he or she gets the reward after doing what is needed. Likewise, if you give a negative consequence, don't let your child talk you out of delivering it. If you later feel what you did was unreasonable or done out of anger, apologize and adjust the consequence accordingly. However, if it is a reasonable consequence, let it stand.

Show empathy. Let your child know you understand that he or she might feel angry or sad, especially when you must give a large negative consequence. It can make all the difference in how your child accepts it.

Let your behavior match the consequence. Be pleasant and enthusiastic when giving positive consequences. Let children know when they've accomplished something, especially if the positive behavior or skill they used is one they haven't been able or willing to use in the past. Be sure to praise even small steps toward progress. When giving negative consequences, stay calm, don't yell, and use a firm but matter-of-fact voice tone. Yelling and screaming are not effective ways to give negative consequences. When you blow up, kids don't hear your words; they only hear your anger. Be a good role model when it comes to dealing with frustration, anger, and upset.

Don't give group consequences. This is rarely effective. It is highly unlikely that every child in the group is demonstrating the same behavior or will be motivated by the same consequence. It's best to find individual consequences that will motivate each child.

Warnings

"If you don't stop that, I'll take your game away."

"You know you're not supposed to act that way. Next time, I'm going to ground you."

"If I have to tell you one more time, I'll...."

Warnings like these don't work. In fact, they actually train your children to do exactly what you don't want them to do! Kids quickly figure out that you won't follow through on what you threaten to do. They know it's okay to ignore your warnings and keep on misbehaving. Your parenting and whatever consequences you may be using become ineffective.

If you tell your child you will take away a game for certain misbehavior, and the misbehavior occurs, then take the game away. This helps your child understand what behaviors are acceptable and which ones are unacceptable. It also helps your children make the connection between their behaviors and the consequences they receive. Otherwise, what you say is confusing and encourages "limit testing" by your child: "I think I can get away with it again. Mom's warned me three times and so far nothing's happened."

Positive Consequences

Positive consequences can be a parent's best friend because they can increase the kinds of behaviors parents want their children to use. However, positive consequences sometimes can be a problem if they are used too often or are mistakenly given following a negative behavior. Generally, positive consequences are considered to be privileges or rewards — things kids like or enjoy. Therefore, when we use the term "privileges," we mean any type of positive consequence children can earn that will motivate them to do more positive things!

Using positive consequences is one way to increase the amount of time children spend doing positive things. When you give positive consequences, your kids feel your teaching is fair and they are more motivated to cooperate with you. They begin to understand that using the behaviors you are trying to teach them will earn things they want and like. In addition to changing your child's behavior for the better, giving praise and positive consequences can help you build a good relationship with your child. Children see parents who balance negative and positive consequences as more fair and reasonable. Parents who use a variety of positive consequences are more pleasant and effective, and kids are more likely to listen to them.

Bribes vs. Positive Consequences

Some parents initially see giving positive consequences to children as a form of bribery, or a payoff, for doing what kids are expected to do. But there are important differences between bribes and positive consequences. Parents sometimes give bribes or rewards to children in exchange for a promise to improve their behavior. For example, a dad who allows his son to use the car if he promises to improve his grades on the next report card has given a bribe, not a positive consequence. Bribery also occurs when a reward is given as a way to stop inappropriate behavior. For example, giving a child a candy bar to stop his whining in the grocery store checkout lane is a bribe. A parent in this situation might feel forced to do anything to stop the child's negative behavior: *"Okay, you can have the candy. Just shut up!"* The bottom line is the child is rewarded for bad behavior. Even though the candy did work to silence the child, guess what will happen the next time the parent is in the grocery checkout lane? Right — the child will whine and demand a candy bar. The child has learned whining can get him what he wants. He has learned to expect a reward before he behaves as his parent wants.

Positive consequences should be contingent on positive behavior. That is, children should receive positive consequences only *after* they use appropriate behavior or do what a parent asks (Grandma's rule). Remember, positive consequences should not be awarded for a promise of better behavior in the future or to stop negative behavior — those are bribes.

Positive Consequences That Work

Not every child will respond to the same positive consequences in the same way, because something that is a reward for one child may not be a reward for another. The list on the next page suggests a variety of privileges that parents have used as consequences with their children. Using these examples as a guide, identify what your child likes to do and write those preferences on a sheet of paper. Keep the list handy until you have a pretty good idea which positive consequences will work best with your child.

Pairing Positive Consequences with Behavior

Pairing the "right" consequences with positive behaviors increases the chances your child will continue those behaviors. By "right" consequences, we mean those that are strongly linked to the positive behavior. For example, if your son would rather play video games than do his homework, you can reward him with 15 minutes of extra screen time when he does sit down after school or dinner and finishes his homework. You have linked that consequence in a positive

PRIVILEGE LIST

Activities — What everyday activities does your child like to do: Playing video and computer games, texting their friends, playing baseball, watching sitcoms, baking cookies, or reading?

Possessions — What kinds of material articles does your child like: A cell phone, special clothing or other apparel, cosmetics, music CDs, movie DVDs, books, baseball cards, video games, comic books, or toys?

Special Activities — What special activities does your child enjoy: Going swimming, visiting the zoo, going to a movie, or having a friend stay overnight?

Special Foods — What are your child's favorite foods and beverages: Popcorn, ice cream bars, pizza, cola, candy, waffles, granola bars, or fruit juice? (Never use meals as a positive consequence or withhold them as a negative consequence. Children have the right to proper nutrition and they should never have to earn their breakfast, lunch, or dinner.)

People — Who does your child like to spend time with: You, friends, grandparents, or cousins? Relationships with family, friends, mentors, teachers, coaches, and others who are important to children are some of the most powerful reinforcers you can use. So use them as often as possible!

Attention — What specific kinds of verbal and physical attention from you and others does your child like: Hugs, smiles, time with you, compliments, high-fives, thumbs up, or praise?

Other Rewards — Is there anything else your child likes, is interested in, or would like to spend time doing? Is there a favorite hobby or some experience he or she has wanted to do but hasn't yet done?

way to the behavior that is giving him trouble. When children know using a certain behavior will earn a certain reward, that consequence becomes a powerful behavior-change tool. The following examples show some possible pairings of behaviors and consequences and the reason why the pairing can be effective.

Behavior: Your 16-year-old daughter comes home on time three weekends in a row after earning a negative consequence for missing her curfew.

Positive Consequence: Extend her curfew by 30 minutes for one night.

Reason: Following the curfew rule is rewarded by a later curfew.

Behavior: Without being told to do so, your 10-year-old puts on his pajamas and gets ready for bed without complaining or whining.

Positive Consequence: Let him play or read quietly in bed for an extra 15 minutes before turning out the light.

Reason: Following the bedtime routine without being prompted earns him more time before "lights out."

Behavior: Your 7-year-old and 11-year-old, both of whom often argue and don't get along, play nicely together in the backyard for an hour.

Positive Consequence: Fix them some popcorn while they watch a movie they've chosen together with your approval.

Reason:	The consequence extends the cooperative interaction between the siblings and rewards them for getting along with each other.

Negative Consequences

When children misbehave, they should receive negative consequences. As we know, consequences help change behavior. If negative consequences are given in a firm, fair, and consistent manner, they will be effective at reducing your child's misbehaviors.

Negative consequences should not be confused with punishment. Punishment involves some kind of adverse activity that causes physical pain (spanking) or deprives children of something they have a fundamental right to have (sending a child to bed without dinner). Activities like these have only one purpose — to punish. Negative consequences, on the other hand, are humane, not harmful, and focus on teaching. There are two kinds of negative consequences for misbehavior — taking away a privilege and adding chores.

Loss of a Privilege

The negative consequence of taking away a privilege is usually effective with most children because it often can be directly tied to the behavior that earned the consequence. For example, if your teenage daughter comes home an hour late, you may remove part of the privilege of going out (have her come home an hour earlier the next time she goes out). If this is a frequent problem, she may lose the privilege of going out altogether. For example, you could say to your daughter, *"Sarah, because you were one hour late getting home, you can't go out at all tomorrow night."* Similarly, if your two sons are arguing about which TV show to watch, you can shut off the TV until they settle their differences, or they could lose TV the rest of the evening. If this is the first time the boys have had this problem, you could say, *"Boys, you're arguing about which show to watch. Please shut the TV off until you can calmly come to me with a solution."*

Adding Chores

Besides working well as a behavior-shaping tool, the negative consequence of adding chores is an effective way to teach responsibility and other important social skills. Chores take time and effort from your children, time they could spend playing, being with friends, or doing something enjoyable. Children begin to learn that the way to avoid having to spend time on extra chores that take them away from activities they like is to stop using the negative behavior that led to the added chore.

Ideally, chores should relate directly to the problem behavior, while also addressing the skill the child needs to work on. For example, you have instructed your son to take his shoes off when he comes home from baseball practice so he doesn't track dirt into the house. When he fails to follow this instruction, you can tell him to vacuum the carpet. This way, he's doing a chore that's related to the problem behavior and working on the skill of "Following Instructions."

The process of adding chores is simple. For example, your daughter is supposed to pick up her clothes instead of leaving them on the floor. If she doesn't follow this instruction, you can have her gather the dirty clothes from every bedroom and put them in the hamper. Adding this chore is a way to correct her behavior and teach the skills of "Taking Responsibility" and "Following Instructions."

Coming up with a related consequence isn't always easy. Nor is it necessary. Chores don't always have to be related to the negative behavior to be effective. For example, if your daughter comes home late on a weekend night, you can let her know she will have to earn the privilege of going out the following weekend by finishing all her regular chores, plus an extra task, on time during the week. This consequence should help reduce the behavior problem of being late even though having her complete her chores on time is not related to breaking curfew.

The following examples show some possible pairings of added chores and children's problem behaviors:

Behavior: Your daughter breaks her glasses for the third time in the last three months.

Chore: She must earn money to buy new glasses by taking responsibility for walking, grooming, and feeding the family dog.

Reason: Taking care of the family pet is a way of learning to be responsible.

Behavior: Your son borrows the car and returns it on time. However, the inside of the car is littered with food and candy wrappers.

Chore: You decide he has to clean the inside and outside of the car before he can call or spend time with his friends.

Reason: Cleaning the car teaches him to be considerate of others.

Behavior: Your sons are arguing about who gets to use the computer.

Chore: Their consequence is to fold a load of laundry together while working out a solution on how to take turns using the computer.

Reason: Working together helps the brothers learn to get along.

Behavior: Your son and daughter are yelling at each other about who last put away the clean dishes.

Chore: They have to put away the dishes together for the next three days.

Reasons: Repeatedly doing chores together helps them learn and practice working and getting along with each other.

On the next page is a list of chores you can use as negative consequences for older children and teenagers. Make sure the added chores you choose are different from the routine chores kids normally do as part of their family responsibilities and aren't reinforcing to the child (something the child likes to do). For example, younger kids might enjoy doing a chore with another person instead of by themselves.

It's up to you to decide how often a chore should be done, and to define exactly what your child should do. Take into account his or her age and ability. Also, adjust the consequences to fit the severity of the problem behavior. Remember to use the smallest consequence necessary to change the behavior.

One variation parents tell us works well is the "chore jar." Parents write various chores on small pieces of paper and put them in a jar. When a child misbehaves, the parents have him or her select a chore from the chore jar. This makes it easier for parents because the consequences are readily available.

CHORES THAT TAKE A SHORT TIME

- Folding laundry
- Putting laundry away
- Making another family member's bed
- Vacuuming one (or several) rooms
- Raking part of the yard
- Mowing the grass
- Taking out the trash
- Collecting the trash from throughout the house
- Helping a brother or sister with his or her chores
- Dusting furniture
- Washing some windows in your home

- Sweeping the porch
- Washing the car
- Vacuuming the car
- Washing trash cans
- Sweeping the garage floor
- Helping a brother or sister put toys away
- Washing, drying, or putting away dishes
- Sweeping the kitchen floor
- Polishing silverware
- Cleaning the pantry and taking extra food items to a food bank
- Cleaning the refrigerator

Parents should tell kids ahead of time about the chore jar and how it will work. Many parents use the chore jar for common misbehaviors like talking back or not following instructions right away. Some parents have their children put the slip of paper into a second jar after the chore has been completed. Then, when the first jar is empty, another chore jar is ready to use.

Is It Really a Negative Consequence?

Sometimes, parents make the mistake of assuming a consequence is negative when it isn't. Look at the effect a consequence has on the behavior you want to change. If the behavior stops or decreases in frequency, you've given a negative consequence. If the behavior continues or occurs more often, you've either given a positive consequence, or the size, immediacy, importance, frequency, and/or contingency of the consequence isn't right.

For example, one mother said her 6-year-old continually fidgeted and talked in church. One day during the service, she told him that if he kept misbehaving, he couldn't come with her to church next time. He continued to fidget like crazy and talked his head off, because he didn't want to be in church to begin with! His mother's "negative consequence" of not letting him come to church with her in the future actually encouraged more problem behaviors. The behavior she wanted to stop (fidgeting) increased because going to church was not as important to her son as not going. She had actually given her son a positive consequence by forgetting that consequences need to be important to the child.

Here's what we suggested to this mother. She could:

Remove a privilege: If her son fidgets and talks in church, he can't play with his friend afterwards.

Add a chore: If he fidgets and talks in church, he has to help clean up the pews after the service.

The mother tried both methods, and they worked. After a few minor prompts, the young boy learned to sit quietly in church.

Pay close attention to how a consequence affects the behavior you want to change. If the problem behavior begins to decrease or stops altogether, you have given an effective negative consequence. Remember to vary even an effective consequence so it holds a child's interest and attention.

The Snowball Effect

One problem with negative consequences is that parents sometimes lose sight of when to stop giving them. If one consequence doesn't work, parents often try another that is bigger and harsher. When the problem behavior continues, frustrated parents begin piling negative consequences on top of negative consequences. This can spiral out of control, causing consequences to reach excessively large proportions. We call this the "snowball effect."

Here's an example:

When Amy refused to clean her bedroom, her dad took away her telephone privileges for a weekend. When her room was messy the next day, she lost a week of TV privileges. Amy again refused to pick up her room, and her father got

---

"CLEAN THE SLATE"

A good strategy to use when consequences get out of hand is to "clean the slate." This means all negative consequences a child has earned are suspended — along with all of the child's privileges. The child then has the opportunity to earn back a limited number of privileges throughout the day or the next day by doing chores or using positive behavior you specify.

$\longrightarrow$

---

angrier and more frustrated. So he added another month without phone privileges, another week without TV, and told her she couldn't come out of her room until it was spotless.

The list of negative consequences had become an avalanche! In three days, this girl lost just about all communication with the outside world! She also lost every motivation to improve her behavior. This is a good example of how a parent can get carried away with giving ineffective negative consequences when a child misbehaves. Anger and a lack of planned consequences led to the snowball effect. To prevent this situation, don't fire off a string of increasingly harsh negative consequences when you are stressed, frustrated, or upset. Instead, step back, calm down, and look at the effects of the consequence you are using to address the child's behavior. Then change the consequence if necessary, but don't let it snowball out of control. Bigger and "badder" is not necessarily better. And remember: You are also modeling for your child how to deal with frustration and anger. Since the consequences the father gave in our example were unreasonable (and impossible for him to enforce and for his daughter to carry out), we suggested he go back, talk to Amy, apologize for losing his cool, give her a chance to apologize to him, and set up the following plan:

First, Dad should encourage Amy's positive behaviors while she cleans her room as a step toward mending their relationship. He could break the consequence into "doable" parts and have Amy earn back some of her phone privileges. For example, after spending 20 minutes of following instructions, accepting criticism, and staying on task cleaning her bedroom, Amy could earn back 15 minutes of phone time. Second, Amy can help Dad clean the garage because she refused to do what her father asked and to prove she is able to follow instructions well enough to earn back her freedom around the house. If she completes both parts of the plan, Amy eventually gets all of her privileges back. To help Amy consistently keep her room clean, we helped the father find a way to use Grandma's rule — each day that Amy's room is neat and tidy, she gets to use the phone and watch her favorite TV show. She can't use the privileges until her chores are completed.

This practical solution worked. Amy's room was not spotless, but it was clean much more often than it was dirty. And Dad knew exactly what consequence to use, whether the room was clean or dirty, and when to use consequences. Dad learned how to avoid the snowball effect and still give a negative consequence that worked.

Summary

Appropriate consequences teach children successful ways to behave. They can help strengthen positive behaviors and reduce negative behaviors. There are five variables you should consider in order to make consequences effective: importance, immediacy, frequency, size, and contingency.

The more you effectively use positive consequences, the more likely you are to see positive behavior. The most powerful rewards for children can be praise and positive attention from you. If you focus on the good things your kids do, you'll find that positive consequences work!

Finding effective, appropriate negative consequences can be a challenge for parents, but it can be done with time and effort. If your children misbehave, remember to stay calm, don't act out of anger or frustration, and do one of the following — remove all or part of a privilege, or add a chore. Be logical, fair, and consistent, and avoid letting negative consequences snowball into ridiculous and ineffective territory.

Consequences are not a magical cure-all for child behavior problems. **They are effective only when you use them consistently and over time as part of your teaching approach.** Make sure the consequences you use are varied enough so they stay new and fresh to your children. Outside of a strong relationship with your child, consequences are the most powerful tools you have to bring about lasting changes in how he or she behaves.

☞ CHAPTER REVIEW

What should you use to help change behavior?

Positive and negative consequences.

What are the two types of negative consequences?

Taking away privileges and assigning small work chores.

What are the five variables of effective consequences?

Importance, immediacy, frequency, size, and contingency.

☆ ACTION PLAN

1. Take some time to answer the following questions:

   • What is the most important thing you learned in this chapter?

   • What do you plan to do differently as a result of what you've learned?

2. With the help of your children, create a "joy jar" of positive consequences and a "job jar" of negative consequences that you can use to respond to good behavior or misbehavior.

   • Gather the material you will need: two empty plastic jars or tins with lids, colorful construction paper, tape or glue, colored pens or pencils.

   • Bring the family together and ask the children to make a list of all the things they really like (positive consequences). (Suggest that it include lots of things that make them happy but don't have to be purchased — for example, visiting a special friend, extra time on the telephone, or staying up past their bedtime.) Next, have them list the things they don't like to do (negative consequences).

   • Have the children decorate and label the jars and write their positive and negative consequences on slips of paper. (Skip decorating the jar if your children are too old to enjoy that.) If you want to have different consequences for each child, use different colored slips of paper for each child.

- Make the activity fun by offering snacks. Keep it short — no more than 20 minutes — and meet again if you don't finish the jars.

- After the jars are completed, give each child a positive consequence from the joy jar.

Q&A
FOR PARENTS

Q **I've tried every type of negative consequence I can think of and none of them work. What now?**

A The effectiveness of consequences can depend on the quality of your relationship with your child and how well you have incorporated teaching into your relationship. For example, if you have relied on punishment in the past, your child may see negative consequences as an extension of that previous punishment. Try emphasizing positive consequences when you see appropriate behavior, and focus on modeling the behavior you want to see from your child. Talk to your child at a neutral time about the behavior you want to see — not just when your child has misbehaved. Improving your relationship in these ways should make negative consequences work better in the future.

Q **You talk about using "special snacks" as a consequence, but I don't agree with my kids having anything other than fruit for snacks, and they get fruit anytime they want. What am I supposed to do?**

A That's fine! Simply use other types of consequences. Our lists of consequences are just suggestions you can modify to suit your family's circumstances and beliefs.

Q **Shouldn't kids do some things just because they're supposed to? My parents never rewarded me for doing chores; they just tanned my hide if I didn't!**

A Maybe kids should, but sometimes they don't. Consequences can encourage kids to start doing these things. Once kids learn and continue these behaviors, you can decrease or eliminate the consequences you give your child for doing routine chores.

Q **The only positive consequence my teen wants is new gym shoes, and I can't afford to buy them.**

A You don't have to purchase things for your kids when they do something well. In this instance, you could praise your son when he does well, and occasionally offer him opportunities to do extra chores to earn money he could put toward new gym shoes.

Q **I don't have enough money to keep giving my child some of these positive consequences. What am I supposed to do?**

A Use consequences that don't cost money (see the list on the next page). There are many activities and privileges that can be used as effective consequences that don't involve money — time spent with friends, a trip to the park, extra TV time, etc. Remember, your time and attention are the most powerful consequences in your child's life.

Rewards That Cost No Money

- Staying up late
- Having a messy room for a day
- Staying out later
- Listening to music
- Having a friend over
- Sleeping downstairs or in a tent outside
- Going over to a friend's house
- Choosing a TV program
- Having extra TV time
- Picking an outing
- Playing a video game
- Doing one less regular chore
- Having study time in the bedroom or with the music on
- Having Mom or Dad read a story at night
- Staying up late to read
- Playing a game with big brother or sister
- Using the car

- Sleeping in late
- Having extra phone time
- Having friends over for a cookout
- Eating special snacks
- Going to the mall with friends on the weekend
- Going to the library, pet store, park, etc.
- Having an extra night out with friends
- Getting permission for a special event
- Eating snacks in the family room
- Having extra time on the computer
- Riding a bike or fishing
- Having an indoor picnic
- Choosing the breakfast cereal
- Going window shopping

$\Rightarrow$

Chapter 5
Using Reasons to Encourage Improvement

"Why do I have to do the dishes?"
"Why can't I stay up later tonight?"
"Why won't you let me text my friends?"

"Why" is a word that's a big part of most children's vocabulary. Sometimes, parents feel bombarded with the word. When your kids constantly question your decisions, it can leave you feeling irritated, frustrated, or angry. You may feel your authority is being challenged or your children are just trying to drive you crazy! But it's normal for all people, especially kids, to ask and want to know *"Why?"* Children aren't plotting your demise; rather, they simply don't understand your point of view. Giving logical reasons to children can help them understand more and debate less.

Let's bring this to your level for a minute. For example, let's say your boss asks you to work late on a project without telling you why. You might be annoyed and maybe even feel like you're being punished. However, if your boss explains to you that the project deadline has been moved up from tomorrow afternoon to first thing in the morning, then you understand the request better and can comply without as many negative feelings and thoughts. The same holds true for kids. So make it easier on yourself and your child and head off a case of the "whys" by giving reasons up front.

What Are Reasons?

Reasons are statements that help people make and understand the connection between their behavior and what happens to others and themselves as a result of their behavior. Reasons are a part of many parenting skills presented later in this book, and they can be used anytime it is necessary to teach a child why it is important to use certain behaviors and skills in specific situations.

There is a difference between "general reasons" and "child-oriented reasons," the kind you will learn to use with children. These reasons are geared specifically to a child's point of view or understanding. For example, a general reason for cleaning one's room might be, *"Cleaning your room helps to keep it neat for when guests come over."* A child-oriented reason would be something like, *"When you keep your room clean, I'm more likely to let you have your friends over to play."*

Why Use Child-Oriented Reasons

Giving children reasons for using certain behaviors increases the likelihood they will make the connection between their actions and the consequences (both positive and negative) of those actions. Reasons help children understand they may be able to control what happens to them simply by changing how they behave. If kids see the benefits of a positive behavior to themselves or others, they are more likely to behave that way in the future. Similarly, if they understand the personal disadvantages of a negative behavior, they will be less likely to engage in that misbehavior.

Other benefits of using child-oriented reasons include:

- Your children view you as being fair when you use reasons, especially when you are teaching them. Reasons help children understand that what you are trying to teach them will have a direct effect on them. Children learn how certain behaviors help or hurt them personally.

- Reasons enhance children's moral development. When you point out to children how their behavior affects others, you are helping them become self-reflective while nurturing their ability to be more other-centered.

- When you take the time to give reasons, you are helping to build the relationship between you and your child. Children see you as patient, caring, and truly interested in helping them.

Types of Child-Oriented Reasons

There are three types of reasons you can give your children. You can explain how their behavior will benefit them, how it will create a negative outcome for them, or how it will affect others. The type of reason you use will depend upon the age or maturity of your child and the behavior you are trying to either encourage or change.

Benefit-to-Child

This type of reason lets children know how a behavior will directly benefit them. *("If you save the money from your paper route, then you'll be able to buy a new bike"* or *"If you help me clear the table, you can go outside and play with your friends after dinner.")* You will often use this type of reason with a young or immature child who has not gotten beyond the "me-centered" way of thinking.

Negative-Outcome

These reasons point out to children an undesirable outcome for their actions. *("When you argue with your friends, they might not want to be around you.")* There are times when negative-outcome reasons are necessary. They are especially effective when you need to point out serious outcomes, such as those related to safety. *("If you wander away from me at the mall, you might get lost"* or *"If you have too many other kids in the car with you, you might get distracted and have an accident.")* As a general guideline, however, don't overuse negative-outcome reasons because you may appear to be nagging. Whenever possible, phrase negative-outcome reasons in a positive way. For example, if you say, *"Don't stay up too late or you'll be tired tomorrow,"* you can add, *"If you go to bed earlier, you'll feel more energetic in the morning."*

Concern-for-Others

When you use this type of reason, you are trying to get children to imagine themselves in someone else's shoes. You are asking children to see the situation from another point of view, which gives them an opportunity to think about how they might feel if someone did the same thing to them.

("When you call Jamar that name, you make him feel bad.") This type of reason is especially helpful for developing morals and values. *("When you help your brother with his homework, you show him you care about him and want to help him do well in school.")* You may not use this type of reason with very young children, but eventually you will want them to start thinking about how their actions affect others. Using this type of reason helps children develop empathy as they grow older.

Examples of Child-Oriented Reasons

Here are examples of how each type of reason could be used in the same situations:

Benefit-to-Child

1. *"Good job, Sandy. You accepted my criticism and changed your skirt. When you can accept criticism, it shows me you're growing up and able to handle more responsibilities."*

2. *"Diondre, because you didn't do what I asked the first time, you have lost an hour of your screen time. When you follow instructions, you can get back to what you were doing sooner."*

3. *"Carlos, the next time you feel like you're getting angry, take a few deep breaths. If you do that, it can help avoid making things worse."*

Negative-Outcome

1. *"Good job, Sandy. You accepted my criticism and changed your skirt. Not accepting criticism usually leads to more criticism."*

2. *"Diondre, because you didn't do what I asked the first time, you have lost an hour of your screen time. When you don't follow instructions, you lose the opportunity to do the things you want."*

3. *"Carlos, the next time you feel like you're getting angry, take a few deep breaths. When you lose control, you just get into more trouble."*

Concern-for-Others

1. *"Good job, Sandy. You accepted my criticism and changed your skirt. When you can accept criticism, it makes me very proud of you."*

2. *"Diondre, because you didn't do what I asked the first time, you have lost an hour of your screen time. When you follow instructions, it shows you respect our family rules."*

3. *"Carlos, the next time you feel like you're getting angry, take a few deep breaths. If you do, you won't blow up and hurt someone's feelings."*

When to Use Reasons

You should use reasons with all the different parenting skills you will learn in this book; for example, when you're teaching self-control *("When you argue with me instead of doing what I've asked, you end up losing your phone privileges.")*, or when you're correcting misbehavior *("When you take the car without asking for permission, I'm less likely to trust you with the car in the future.")*. But the best time to talk to children about reasons is when you are teaching about behavior at neutral or positive times. This is when your child is most willing to listen to you. If you have talked during calm moments about the reasons why some behaviors are acceptable and others are not, your child will be more likely to listen to reasons when he or she needs correction or is angry and upset.

Giving Effective Reasons

If you tell a child, *"Pick up your room because I said so,"* you might say you've given a reason. But it's doubtful such a reason will be successful in influencing your child's behavior in the future. Effective reasons have certain qualities that make them work.

Use reasons that are individualized and personal to kids.

The reasons that seem to work best with children are those that point out something that is important to them personally. If you have a child who loves sports, use sports-related reasons. *("If you learn how to follow instructions, your soccer coach may notice and let you play more.")* If you have a teen daughter who wants to get a weekend job, show how a particular skill could help her land a job. *("Knowing how to introduce yourself gives a potential employer a good first impression of you.")* These reasons not only show benefits to the child, but also may act as motivators.

Be as brief and specific as possible.

If you make reasons too long, you'll appear to be lecturing and your child may tune you out. Also, don't give a list of reasons; one is usually enough. If you say, *"When you follow instructions, you show others you are trustworthy and you may be seen as a leader by your teacher, or you might*

85

get your work done early and have some free time," you run the risk of the child not remembering any of your reasons.

Make reasons convincing and believable.

For some children, the reasons you give are what they will expect to happen. Instead of saying, *"Share with others and then everyone will like you,"* say something more realistic like, *"When you share with others, they'll probably share with you."* To make your reason believable, also consider the child's age. This reason would not make much sense to a young child: *"When you are able to follow instructions, you might get a higher paying job when you grow up."* Instead, it makes more sense to a young child if you say, *"When you follow instructions, you will have more time to play."*

Use "possibility" words.

Including "possibility" words can help a child understand the reason for using a skill or behavior while minimizing the impression he is being promised something in return. Phrases such as, *"you are more likely"* or *"in the future you might"* help a child understand that the reason for using the skill is not an absolute in all situations. This may cut down on instances where a child feels like something was promised but not delivered or comments such as, *"But you said if I did this, I would get to...."*

Point out natural and logical outcomes for a certain behavior.

Children need to learn that some behaviors have natural outcomes that aren't necessarily influenced by you. *("Going to bed on time makes it easier for you to get up on time and feel good in the morning.")* Be sure to make natural and logical outcomes age-appropriate for the child. Also, keep in mind that children often need reasons to do what you ask of them that are more motivating than natural and logical ones.

Use reasons that show how a skill can be generalized (or easily transferred) to other situations.

Children need to see how their behavior affects others outside their own home. *("When you greet others politely, people see you as a nice person.")* When you can, use a general term like "people" instead of "I" to help with generalization. Say, *"When you take responsibility and follow through on instructions, teachers and friends see you are trustworthy and know they can count on you"* instead of *"When you take responsibility and follow through on instructions, I know I can count on you."*

Use reasons often.

It takes a lot of teaching and practice before children learn what we want them to know — using table manners, doing chores on time, etc. It's the same with reasons. You may need to patiently give a reason several times in similar situations before children begin to understand why they should or should not behave in a certain way.

Focus on the positive.

While it is true unpleasant things can result when children misbehave, we don't want kids to be motivated primarily by the fear that bad thing will happen. Rather, children should be motivated by the positive results of doing things well. So, limit how often you use reasons like *"You'll get hurt"* or *"You'll get into trouble."* Instead, use reasons that show your children how they, and others, benefit from doing something well. Use reasons like, *"If you get your homework done right away, you'll have more time to do fun things on the computer."*

Summary

There will be many times every day when you can use reasons with your child, especially during the teaching opportunities you will read about later in this book. When you give reasons to children, they are more likely to understand your point of view and why it is important to use certain behaviors and not use others. Reasons also help children make a connection between their behavior and what happens to them as a result. Realize, though, that reasons alone seldom change behavior. Teaching plus reasons plus consequences is the best formula for changing behavior.

☞ CHAPTER REVIEW

Give the definition of child-oriented reasons.

These reasons show children the relationship between their behavior and what happens to them and others as a result of their behavior. They are related to a child's point of view or understanding.

Why is it important to give child-oriented reasons?

Children are more likely to do what parents ask them to do.

What are the different types of reasons?

Reasons that show benefit to the child, a negative outcome to the child, and concern for others.

 ACTION PLAN

1. Take some time to answer the following questions:

    *   What is the most important thing you learned in this chapter?

    *   What do you plan to do differently as a result of what you learned?

2. As part of the conversation at your next family meal, ask your children to share:

    *   How they have benefited from making and using the joy and job jars.

    *   Reasons why they shouldn't neglect doing their chores or homework.

    *   Reasons why it's important for family members to listen to and help each other.

Praise and encourage your children as they join the conversation. Explain why you are having them share their ideas at the family meal.

Q&A
FOR PARENTS

Q **Am I supposed to give my children reasons for everything I want them to do?**

A No, children would probably tune you out if you gave reasons for everything you want them to do. When you want to increase positive behaviors your children don't do routinely, reasons can be used more frequently at first to help get children started with using unfamiliar behaviors. As the child masters the behavior, reasons can be faded away.

Q **When you give reasons to kids, aren't you just giving them an opportunity to argue and debate?**

A Giving reasons should decrease the chances of this happening because you've already answered the child's "why" question upfront. Remember, you don't have to give several reasons; just give one child-oriented reason and move on.

Q **What's wrong with telling kids to do something just because we are parents telling them to do it?**

A There's nothing wrong with this kind of statement. But giving children reasons is much more effective than giving subtle threats or warnings. It saves you time and gets kids to be more cooperative.

Q Will giving reasons to children really help them behave?

A Research shows that giving children reasons helps them develop self-discipline, which improves their behavior and cuts down on conflict.

Q Should I give reasons to preschool and young children who might not understand them?

A Yes! But make your reasons are age-appropriate and use words young children understand. They might not comprehend everything you say, but over time, they will begin to understand.

Encouraging Good Behavior and Preventing Problems

Recognizing and praising your children's positive behavior often and appropriately may be the most important skill you learn as a parent. Besides strengthening your relationship with your children, encouraging and praising good behavior nurtures and is a powerful expression of your love for them.

Praise is a wonderful thing, especially in a parent-child relationship. It is an ideal way for parents to show their children they are accepted and appreciated, which is very important to promoting children's growth and willingness to cooperate with parents. The only bad thing about praise is that most parents don't use it often enough as a teaching tool.

Unfortunately, some of you may not have experienced a lot of encouragement or praise yourselves while growing up.

Giving words of praise to your children may feel awkward and unfamiliar to you. Some may simply use praise as a way to compliment children and not as a parenting skill to encourage children's good behavior. Parents of defiant or strong-willed children also tell us they have a difficult time finding behaviors that are worthy of praise. So they tend to focus on their son's or daughter's negative behaviors or recognize only major accomplishments.

In Chapter 6, you will learn how to overcome these obstacles and others by using Effective Praise. It will explain how parents who want a more pleasant, loving family atmosphere must focus on looking for positive behaviors to praise, giving consistent support, acceptance, and encouragement, and recognizing the small changes in a child's behavior that show progress.

To change misbehavior, children must learn what they need to do or say in new or problem situations. As we will explain in Chapter 7, parents can help their children improve on how they respond to situations where they've experienced problems in the past and new situations by using Preventive Teaching before those situations occur. Preventive Teaching is a parenting tool that helps kids learn and practice skills before they need to use them, increasing their chances for success and preventing problems.

There are many rewards to using Preventive Teaching. For children, the payoff is they are better prepared to respond positively and appropriately in many situations because they have learned what to do and practiced it beforehand. Parents are rewarded in knowing they have provided their children with skills that will help them make good decisions, find success, and stay out of trouble. Another benefit to parents is they spend less time and energy correcting misbehaviors because they have prevented many of those behaviors by teaching their kids positive skills.

Another way to encourage good behavior and build character is to use charts with younger children and contracts with older children. Chapter 8 will show you how to set goals by using child-friendly charts and contracts that clearly spell out the positive behaviors you want your children to use as well as the benefits they can gain by demonstrating those behaviors. They can be fun to use and provide powerful incentives to children for using good behavior.

As you read the following chapters, keep in mind you cannot change your children's behaviors or teach them new behaviors overnight. Think of praise and the teaching and practice of new skills as being like water flowing on a rock; eventually, behavior will change and be reshaped, just as the water will change the shape of the rock. It will take time, but if you use the techniques described in these chapters, you will eventually see positive changes in your children's behavior.

Chapter 6
Praise Is Powerful

P raise encourages children to see themselves and the world around them in a different, more positive light. Not only does praise nurture a sense of self-worth, it also can be a powerful catalyst in improving your relationship with your children. Sincere and enthusiastic praise can help your children grow emotionally, just as food helps them grow physically.

Focus on the Positive

Praise is not a new concept; we're all familiar with it. But many of us don't use it as often as we should. Why? One of the reasons is that we have been conditioned to often see only negatives. It is easy to see what people do wrong. In fact, many companies who focus on customer service believe in the "3:11" rule. This rule predicts a customer who experiences good service at a place of business will probably tell three other people about it. On the other hand, when a customer receives poor service, he or she is likely to spread the word to 11 other people! Bad news travels faster.

Parents also typically focus on children's negative behaviors. Your children's mistakes and shortcomings are easy to spot. One parent we worked with told us, "When I was growing up, the only time I knew I was doing something right was when I didn't hear anything from my parents. But I always heard from them when I did something wrong!" How often have you tiptoed past your children when they were "being good," afraid to interrupt them and bring the good behavior to an end?

Using praise effectively, however, actually has just the opposite effect. If you consistently pay attention to your children's good behavior by using praise, you will notice them repeating that behavior, and problem behavior should decrease over time. When you zero in on as many positive things as you can, your kids will feel better about themselves and about you. The positive attention that comes with praise makes children feel cared for and loved. We have found one thing to be true time and time again — praise helps parents focus on what is good about their children.

How to Use Praise

The easiest way to encourage someone is to say things like, "Fantastic," "Great," or "Keep up the good work." This is what we call **general praise**. It's a quick and easy way to focus on the positive things your kids do. These words show your affection and approval and really encourage your children to do well. It takes little time and effort, and the benefits are great!

You can make general praise even better, however. By adding a couple of steps, you can focus your attention on specific behaviors you would like your child to continue to use in the future. Occasionally adding a reward for those behaviors makes the praise even more powerful. That's why we make a distinction between general praise and what we call **Effective Praise. Effective Praise is praising your child for the specific positive behavior he or she displays.**

When to Use Praise

It takes effort to refocus so we see the good things our children do. Here are three general areas where most opportunities to praise occur:

- **Things your children already do well (and you want them to repeat)**
- **Improvements in behavior**
- **Positive attempts at new skills**

As a parent, you may often feel underappreciated. How would you feel if your children suddenly began noticing all the things you do for them that they usually take for granted? As well as feeling pretty good, you'd probably be willing to do even more for them. In the same way, praising your children for what they already do well is like taking out an insurance policy to guarantee future good behavior. Praise increases the chances they will continue to use the behaviors that draw your positive attention, whether it's getting up on time, cleaning their rooms, or playing a game with a younger brother. You just have to take the time to notice good behaviors.

Next, make sure you recognize when your children are making improvements in their behavior. Praise the small steps along the way — making the bed even if all the blankets aren't tucked in, sweeping the floor even if it's not spotless, or asking for permission even if there's no way you're going to let your teen use the car on a school night.

When children are recognized for the effort they make to improve, they will keep on trying to get better.

Finally, since children don't learn new skills without practice and missteps, they may be more likely to stick with it if you praise them for their positive attempts. For example, when your child brought home his or her first attempt at art from kindergarten, you probably praised your child then and for every improvement from that time on — from the first scribble to coloring inside the lines to the poster that won a school contest. Those first attempts were far from perfect, but your praise and attention encouraged your child to keep trying to master the skill. The same principle applies when children are learning new social skills such as accepting criticism without arguing, admitting mistakes, and offering to help, or life skills such as doing their homework, washing their clothes, and applying for a job. Praise the fact that your child is trying.

The Steps of Effective Praise

Here are the steps of Effective Praise and an example of how it works.

1. Show approval.
2. Describe the positive behavior.
3. Give a reason.
4. Give a positive consequence (optional).

Eric has finished his homework before asking to go outside to play. Here's how his mom might praise him:

1. Show approval.
   "Way to go! Eric, I'm proud of you!"

2. **Describe the positive behavior.**
   "You did all your homework before asking to go outside."

3. **Give a reason.**
   "When you finish your homework early, you have more time to play."

Let's examine the importance of each step of Effective Praise.

STEP 1: Show Approval

Children like it when you say nice things about them (who doesn't?), and they are even more captivated by your approval when it is done with enthusiasm and sincerity. When you combine a praise sign or action (voice inflection, body gesture, and/or facial expression) with an encouraging statement, you give your praise much more meaning and power.

Many different words can convey satisfaction with your child's behavior. And show a little excitement! Use words like, *"Awesome! Terrific! Wow! You're right on target! I love you! I'm impressed! Super! Amazing! That's great! Wonderful! Excellent!"* (Doesn't it make you feel better just saying these words?) Be sure you steer clear of backhanded compliments or sarcasm: *"Well, it's about time you cleaned up your room!"* Your words need to be sincere as well as enthusiastic.

Actions are also powerful ways to show your approval: Hugs, kisses, winks, smiles, thumbs up, high-fives, pats on the shoulder, ruffling their hair, clapping, nodding your head. Showing approval lets your child know you are excited and pleased about what he or she is doing. Ultimately, your child will feel uplifted and enjoy being around you.

STEP 2: Describe the Positive Behavior

After you have shown approval, describe the specific positive behaviors you liked. Make sure your children understand what they did so they can repeat the behavior in the future. Clearly describe what you just saw or heard your child do well. For example, say, *"Sarah, thanks for cleaning up the dishes and helping me put the leftovers away,"* or *"Ryan, I'm glad you washed your hands after you went to the bathroom."* Remember to use words your kids understand. Make your praise brief and to the point. Just let your child know what was done well.

STEP 3: Give a Reason

Children benefit from knowing why a behavior is helpful to them or others. As we discussed in Chapter 5, reasons help kids understand the relationship between their behavior and what happens to them. For example, if your young child volunteers to clean up the family room before guests come over (and then does it), explain why that behavior is helpful: *"Cleaning the family room really saved us a lot of time, and now everything is ready for guests to come over."* If your child is a teenager, you could give a different reason for why helping out is important: *"Helping others is a real plus. If you do that on the job, your boss may consider you for a raise or a promotion"* or *"Since you helped out, we'll have time for a driving lesson."*

Reasons are particularly valuable when they are age-appropriate and spell out the benefits your child may receive, either immediately or in the future. So choose a reason you think will mean the most to your child. And remember to use "possibility" words; they can help a child understand the reason for the skill or behavior without giving the impression that he or she is being promised something in return.

STEP 4: Give a Positive Consequence (optional)

Occasionally, you may want to add a fourth step to Effective Praise — a positive consequence (reward). When you are especially pleased with a certain behavior, or your child has made a big improvement in a certain area, you can reward him or her with a special privilege. Rewards can be large or small; that's up to you. Just make sure the size of the reward fits the behavior you want to encourage. Using a consequence following a behavior increases the likelihood of that positive behavior occurring again.

Examples of Effective Praise

Let's look at some examples of how Effective Praise can be used. In the first example, your teenage son has just arrived home before curfew on a weekend night.

1. **Show approval.**
   "Evan, I'm really proud of you!"
   (Smile and pat your son on the back.)

2. **Describe the positive behavior.**
   "You came home on time."

3. **Give a reason.**
   "When you obey your curfew, it shows me you are responsible and that you can be trusted when you go out with your friends."

4. **Give a positive consequence (optional).**
   "Since you came home on time, you can stay out 30 minutes later next weekend when you go out with your friends."

In this example, your son learned specifically what he did right and why it was so important. You increased the likelihood he will make his curfew the next time he's out.

In the next example, your daughter has ignored some teasing by her brother.

1. Show approval.
"Way to go, Tamika!"

2. Describe the positive behavior.
"You ignored your brother when he teased you about your dress."

3. Give a reason.
"You've shown me that you know how to get along with others even when it's difficult."

4. Give a positive consequence (optional).
"Why don't we see if we can find some earrings of mine that would go nicely with your dress?"

In this last example, your son made a request and calmly accepted your "No" answer.

1. Show approval.
"Eric, nice job!"

(Give a "thumbs up" sign.)

2. Describe the positive behavior.
"When I told you 'No' about going outside to hang with your friends, you took a deep breath and counted to ten to calm down."

3. **Give a reason.**

   "This shows me you're learning how to handle disappointment in a more grown-up way. If you keep it up, I'm more likely to allow you to spend time with your friends."

4. **Give a positive consequence (optional).**

   "Because you did so well with calming down, you can stay outside 15 minutes later tomorrow night."

Does Praise Always Work?

Some parents tell us they praise their children, but it doesn't seem to make any difference in their behavior. Some of these parents focus only on outstanding achievements. They miss many opportunities to notice small, positive steps in the right direction. We asked one dad to look for little things to praise. After he began looking closely for and praising small improvements, he noticed many positive changes in his children's behavior. In addition, he felt he was getting along better with his kids.

Other parents tell us they praise their children often, but it doesn't seem to mean much to them. A mom shared with us that she praised her children all the time, whether they were doing something well or not! After a while, her kids began ignoring her, even walking away. She couldn't understand it. "Isn't praising kids a good thing?" she asked. The problem here was that this mother was trying to boost her children's self-esteem, hoping her constant praise would encourage good behavior. Although a parent's love should always be unconditional, given simply because of who a child is, Effective Praise should be given for what a child does. If this mom wants her praise to improve her children's behavior, she must make it contingent on, or give it after, positive behavior.

Some parents have asked us, *"Why should I praise my kids for things they're supposed to do?"* We answer them with another question: *"Do you like being recognized for the things you do well, regardless of whether you're supposed to do them or not?"* For example, do you like to hear your boss tell you you're doing a good job? Most parents say *"Of course."* Just as praise from a boss can build a positive relationship with employees, praising your children improves family relationships.

Effective Praise should be used frequently, but should be given only after children have earned it. That's why it works! When parents provide praise and encouragement for very specific things their kids have actually done, this attention increases the likelihood these same behaviors will occur again.

Summary

Each of your children gives you something to be happy about. Every child does many things, however small, that deserve praise. Make sure that when you see good behavior, you recognize your children for it.

In interviews with some of the thousands of parents who have completed our parenting classes, they consistently tell us that using Effective Praise has had a lasting impact on their families. Parents find themselves being more positive about their children, and kids, in turn, are more positive about their parents. With Effective Praise, everyone wins.

⟶ CHAPTER REVIEW

What is Effective Praise?

Effective Praise is praising children for the specific positive behaviors they display.

Why is it important to praise specific behaviors?

Children are more likely to know what parents want them to do again and to repeat those behaviors.

What are the steps to Effective Praise?

1. Show approval.
2. Describe the positive behavior.
3. Give a reason.
4. Give a positive consequence (optional).

☆ ACTION PLAN

1. Take some time to answer the following questions:

   - What is the most important thing you learned in this chapter?

   - What do you plan to do differently as a result of what you learned?

2. Make an effort to use the things you learned from this chapter in your family's everyday life. At least once a week, during a family meal, go around the table and ask each family member to praise something about the person sitting to his or her left. The next week, go around the

table to the right. Or, have your children say something nice about a parent after you praise the children.

Another variation could be to have each child talk about something he or she did that week that made the child feel good. Praise children for those behaviors and ask them why they think their actions brought them positive feelings.

Q&A
FOR PARENTS

Q Am I supposed to give my daughter a reward every time she does something right?

A No. Praise with a positive consequence is designed to be used to increase behaviors your child struggles with or doesn't do routinely. You may need to give a positive consequence frequently in the beginning to help your daughter get started on using the positive behavior you want to see. Once your daughter starts using the behavior more often or regularly, you can use verbal praise and leave out the reward.

Q What if my son doesn't do anything I think he should be praised for?

A No one does "everything" wrong. Start looking for little or routine things and/or attempts to use new, positive behaviors. For example, say your son is bouncing a basketball on the kitchen floor and you tell him to stop. If he stops immediately, you can say to him, "Thanks for stopping right away. I really appreciate it when you listen to me." Praise even the smallest sign of progress. This will help your son get headed in the right direction.

Q My child doesn't like to be praised! What should I do?

A Many of us feel uncomfortable either giving or receiving praise. Over time, as you keep using praise, you will begin to feel more comfortable giving it and your child will be more receptive to getting it. As a matter of fact, your child will likely grow to enjoy it! But some children don't like being praised in public, especially in front of friends. If this is the case, save your praise for times when you're alone with your child.

Chapter 7
Teaching to Prevent Problems

ealthy families take lots of preventive measures. They install smoke alarms, get the car tuned up, take children to the doctor for physical exams, and keep a first-aid kit stocked and ready to use. We do all of these precautionary things to prevent potential problems, from a house fire to a scraped knee. While prevention can't eliminate all possible problems, it can often make problems that do happen smaller and easier to deal with. In this chapter, we'll show you how to take the same preventive approach to child behavior problems.

We believe parents should spend time teaching important skills to children before they need to use them. One of the best ways we know of doing this is called **Preventive Teaching.** You've probably used this kind of teaching already — showing your child how to safely cross the street or helping him or her memorize the number to dial in an emergency, or teaching your teen how to drive a car safely or change a tire. In these instances, you anticipated or tried to prevent the problems your children might face, as well as increased their chances for success if those problems came up. With Preventive Teaching, you can do the same with your child's social behavior. **Preventive Teaching is teaching your child what he or she needs to say and do in a future situation and practicing it in advance.** Preparing children by helping them learn appropriate social skills not only helps prevent misbehavior but also can save them from experiencing awkward or embarrassing situations.

When to Use Preventive Teaching

There are two types of situations in which you can use Preventive Teaching:

- **When your child is facing a new situation.**

- **When your child has had difficulty in a past situation that is likely to occur again.**

In each case, the key is to use Preventive Teaching **before** your child faces the new situation or **before** your child faces situations where there have been problems in the past. For example, if your son is going to ask his teacher for an extra credit assignment to bring his grade up, you can use Preventive Teaching to demonstrate how he might ask and how the teacher might respond. Or, if your daughter frequently argues or talks back when you ask her to get off the phone or stop texting, you can use Preventive Teaching before she types another message so she can practice how to respond appropriately to your request. In both examples, Preventive Teaching occurs before the child faces the actual situation. (It's best to use Preventive Teaching when your child is calm and attentive, not right after a misbehavior has occurred or when he or she is upset.)

Of course, the behavior areas you focus on when using Preventive Teaching will vary with each child. But all children can learn something new or improve on behaviors that have caused problems in the past. You may want your young son to learn how to make his own breakfast or how to make his bed. Or, you may want your daughter to improve in areas where she has had difficulties before, like making friends with others or getting to bed on time. For a teen, learning how to appropriately ask for (or refuse) a date or how to apply for a job will definitely come in handy. Or, you may want your teen to improve how he responds in situations where he might lose his temper or when he is confronted by a bully.

Preventive Teaching is a simple concept, but parents usually don't use it as often or in as many situations as they could. Here are some examples of situations in which other parents have used Preventive Teaching. Before their children faced a certain situation, they taught their children how to:

- **Come in promptly from playing when called.**
- **Ask for help filling out a job application.**
- **Say "Hello" when being introduced to guests.**
- **Say "No" if someone offers alcohol.**
- **Prepare and give a speech to classmates.**
- **Ask for items in the store and not just take them.**
- **Say "Okay" with no arguing or complaining when told it's time for bed.**
- **Learn to parallel park the car for the driving test.**

As you think about situations that have caused problems for your children, you may notice misbehaviors cropping up in a number of settings. For example, if your child whines or nags you a lot — whether you're at the store, in the car, or at bedtime — you may realize that being told "No" is what usually starts this negative behavior. Teaching your child how to accept "No" for an answer will help clear up this misbehavior in many other situations. (The steps to that skill and many other useful social skills will be discussed in Chapter 12, and can be incorporated into your Preventive Teaching.)

The Steps of Preventive Teaching

The steps of Preventive Teaching combine giving clear messages and child-oriented reasons with another new step — practice. Practice gives children an opportunity to rehearse how they would use the skill before they get into a real-life situation without having to worry about failing. Practice also allows you to observe and assess how your child is using a skill and to provide guidance and advice when needed.

Let's look at the steps of Preventive Teaching:

1. **Describe the desired behavior.**
2. **Give a reason.**
3. **Practice.**

Here's an example of a Preventive Teaching situation. Carlos is about to go on his first camping trip with his grandparents. On prior visits to their home, he has not always followed their instructions, especially with chores. Here's how his father might prepare him for the trip:

1. Describe the desired behavior.

Dad: *"Carlos, when Grandma or Papi ask you to do a chore, look at them and let them know you heard what they said by saying, 'Okay.' Be sure to do what they asked right away. Then let them know when you're finished."*

2. Give a reason.

Dad: *"If you follow instructions right away, you can go do the things you enjoy sooner."*

3. Practice.

Dad: *"Let's pretend I'm Grandma. I am going to ask you to clean off the picnic table. Carlos, please clean off the table. Now, what are you going to say and do?"*

Carlos: *"Okay, and then I would clean off the table, and let Grandma know when I'm done."*

Dad: *"Great! Now run and have fun. Remember to follow instructions tonight when I call you in from playing with your friends."*

Let's examine the importance of each step of Preventive Teaching.

STEP 1: Describe the Desired Behavior

Before your children can do what you want, they must first know what it is you expect. Be specific and describe the positive behaviors you want them to do. Make sure you use words your child understands. For example: Your daughter argued with you the last time you took her shopping. Before her next shopping trip, you can teach her how to respond when she gets a "No" answer. You might say, *"Sandra, tonight when we go shopping, I might have to say 'No' to buying certain outfits you might want. Remember to look at me and say 'Okay' in a calm voice. If you feel like you're getting upset, take a deep breath or ask for time alone."*

STEP 2: Give a Reason

Reasons explain to a child how new skills and appropriate behaviors are helpful and important as well as how inappropriate behaviors are harmful. If reasons are personal to children, they are more likely to accept what you are teaching. For example, you could say to your daughter before the shopping trip, *"When you raise your voice and get upset with me, it takes away from the time we have to shop and we won't really enjoy the outing"* or *"When you accept 'No,' I'm more likely to compromise on other things."* Sometimes it is difficult to come up with reasons that mean a lot to your child right at that moment. If you find you're stumped and can't think of a reason, ask your child for one. For example, you could say, *"Why do you think things go better when you accept 'No' without arguing?"*

STEP 3: Practice

Knowing *what* to do and knowing *how* to do it are two different things. Any new skill needs to be practiced. You can tell your son how to ride a bicycle, but that hardly will ensure that he can hop right on and take off. Likewise, you can tell your daughter how to refuse a date without hurting the guy's feelings, but she's more likely to be successful if she's had a chance to practice what to do and say. Practice increases the chances that your child will be successful at the new skill.

Children occasionally are reluctant to practice, especially when being taught a new skill. They may feel embarrassed, lack self-confidence, or think practicing is a waste of time. The fact of the matter is practice actually eases embarrassment and raises kids' self-confidence in their abilities when they face the real situation. Encourage them as they practice and use a lot of praise, empathy, and patience.

When practicing with younger children, try to make practice fun, yet realistic. Parents report their young children, in particular, enjoy practicing while playing a game or when they are encouraged to use their imagination. Young children like to pretend and play different roles in the practices. This is a time for you to have fun with them and teach them some skills at the same time. For example, you could teach your son how to follow instructions by having him practice after you show him how to shoot a free throw. Or, discuss and practice how a character in a movie or TV show you're watching together could have calmed down instead of getting angry.

Older children and adolescents can be more of a challenge when it comes to practicing. Avoid talking down to them or sounding too serious; these are definite turn-offs for most teens. With older kids, set up the practice step with words like, *"Show me how you would handle..."* or *"Okay, in the same type of situation, what would you say?"* This gives older children an opportunity to actually demonstrate their ability and gives you a chance to see what they need to improve.

After finishing the practice, praise things your child did well and encourage him or her to work on areas that need improvement. Don't expect perfection the first or even the second time you practice. Children will give you plenty of opportunities to practice again!

If your child is practicing a complex skill or a difficult situation, such as how to deal with a bully or apologize to a teacher, never promise that the actual situation will work out perfectly. Emphasize to your child that he or she is practicing possible ways to handle a situation and that the outcome won't always be the same as the one from the practice. You cannot ensure your children's success in every situation, you can only improve the odds. Practicing various situations gives your child more realistic expectations.

Also, the more types of situations and skills you practice with your children, the more likely they are to succeed in the actual situation. You will be helping them learn more and more ways to solve problems. In the earlier example, you were teaching your daughter how to stay calm when she receives a "No" answer on a shopping trip. When it's time for practice, you might say, *"Okay, Sandra, here's another skill you can use when someone tells you 'No' — how to disagree appropriately. We're at the store and I'm telling you 'No' about a skirt you want. Show me what you'll do and say to stay calm and tell me why you disagree."*

Preventive Prompts

After using Preventive Teaching several times to teach a skill, you may need only to provide a reminder to your child rather than going through all three steps when it comes time for him or her to use the skill. This reminder is called a **preventive prompt.** For example, let's say you and your daughter have practiced how she should accept "No" for an answer a number of times. Before you enter a store, you could say, *"Sandra, if I say 'No' about something, remem-*

ber to stay calm and accept it just like we practiced at home." The purpose of a preventive prompt is to remind your child what she practiced before, just before the situation occurs again.

Examples of Preventive Teaching

Here are some more examples of Preventive Teaching:

A 6-year-old boy frequently gets upset and argues with his mom whenever it's time for him to take a bath. Before bath time, she uses Preventive Teaching to teach him the skill of staying calm.

1. Describe the desired behavior.

Mom: *"Michael, sometimes you argue and get upset with me when it's time for you to take a bath. Instead of fighting with me, I want you to pretend like you're blowing out candles and breathe like this."*

(Mom then shows him how to take and blow out deep breaths.)

2. Give a reason.

Mom: *"By blowing out the pretend candles, you'll be letting me know you're upset but you won't get into trouble like you do when you yell and argue with me. Then when you're finished blowing out all the candles, we can talk about why you're upset, okay?"*

119

3. Practice.

Mom: *"Now, pretend you're upset because I told you it's time to take a bath. Show me how you'd blow out the candles to let me know you're upset."*

(Michael takes a deep breath and pretends to blow out the candles three times.)

Mom: *"That's great! Blow out those candles whenever you feel like you're getting upset. Then we can talk about why you're upset."*

A teenage boy is going to a movie with a girl for the first time. His dad wants to teach him how to be a gentleman when he arrives at her home.

1. Describe the desired behavior.

Dad: *"Okay, Sean, there are a few things I want to talk to you about before you go to the movies with Michelle. First, you've got to get to her house on time and that means taking the 5:20 bus. Next, I want you to introduce yourself to her mom. Shake hands with her and say something like, 'Hi, I'm Sean. It's nice to meet you Mrs. Johnson.' Finally, I want you to be sure to hold the door open for Michelle and let her go first through the door. Okay?"*

Sean: *"Yeah, Dad. I'll be fine. I don't know why you're making such a big deal about this."*

2. Give a reason.

Dad: *"Well, if you make a good impression on her mom, she might let you go to the show with Michelle again. And if you treat Michelle with respect, she might agree to go to another movie with you."*

3. Practice.

Dad: *"Now, let's say that I'm Mrs. Johnson. Show me how you'd introduce yourself when she comes to the door. And remember to look at me and shake my hand."*

(Sean shakes his dad's hand and introduces himself.)

Dad: *"Okay, now pretend I'm Michelle and show me what you'd do when we're ready to leave."*

(Sean gets the door for his dad.)

Dad: *"Very good, Sean. I'm sure Michelle's mom will be impressed. Have a great time."*

A teenage girl is going to a party with some friends and her mother wants to make sure she knows what to do if someone who may have been drinking alcohol offers her a ride home. In this example, Mom asks her daughter upfront to describe the behavior she wants to see, varying the sequence of the steps but still doing effective Preventive Teaching. (Mom might also teach her daughter how to leave a party where underage kids are drinking alcohol.)

1. Describe the desired behavior.

Mom: *"We've talked about this before, Lori, but it's real important so I just want to go over it again before you go out tonight. Do you remember what you can say if someone offers you a ride and you think they've been drinking?"*

Lori: *"Yeah, Mom. I should say, 'You shouldn't drive if you've been drink- ing. Please give me the keys and I'll drive you home.' If they refuse, I shouldn't get in the car. Instead, I should call you on my cell phone."*

Mom: *"Great! Now, what would you do if a bunch of kids start teasing you?"*

Lori: *"I could say, 'I like you guys, but I'm not willing to drink. And I'm cer- tainly not going to get in a car with someone who's been drinking. I like my body parts where they are.'"*

2. Give a reason.

Mom: *"Lori, I know sometimes it's tough, but letting your friends know you won't hang around with them when*

*they drink will help you stay out of
trouble. Underage drinking is illegal
and dangerous. As long as you stay
away from drinking and drugs, I'll
let you go out to parties. Okay?"*

3. Practice.

(In this situation, Lori has already practiced saying what she would say to her friends, so her mother might use a preventive prompt just before she leaves the house.)

Summary

Preventive Teaching promotes gradual behavior changes in areas where your children are having problems and helps prepare them for unfamiliar situations. It can increase your children's self-confidence by showing them they can learn how to change their behaviors and be successful. And, perhaps most importantly, Preventive Teaching allows you and your child to practice skills and work toward goals together. Taking the time to be with your children and showing them you care helps improve relationships, and benefits the whole family.

You can make two lists: one for the areas where your child needs to learn something new, and one for the areas where your child has had problems before. Then use Preventive Teaching with these situations before they occur in the future. After using Preventive Teaching, look carefully for any improvements and praise your kids when they do improve.

👉 CHAPTER REVIEW

What is Preventive Teaching?

Preventive Teaching is teaching your child what he or she needs to do in a future situation and practicing it in advance.

Why is it important to practice?

Children are more likely to be successful and meet their parents' expectations.

What are the steps to Preventive Teaching?

1. Describe the desired behavior.
2. Give a reason.
3. Practice.

⭐ ACTION PLAN

1. Take some time to answer the following questions:
   - What is the most important thing you learned in this chapter?
   - What do you plan to do differently as a result of what you learned?

2. Make an effort to use the steps to Preventive Teaching in your family's everyday life. Have your children learn and practice a different skill each week.

   For example, let's say the skill for the week is showing consideration for others. You can teach this skill to your children while having fun. Plan a summertime campout in the backyard. Before pitching the tent, teach your children how to be considerate of the neighbors by practicing how to let them know earlier in the day that the family will be camping out in the backyard, how to keep their voices down during the night, and how to follow instructions and pick up any trash that may blow into the neighbors' yard during the night.

Here's another example: If you want to teach your children good table manners, challenge them to demonstrate good manners at dinner for six nights in a row. If they are successful, let them have a pizza party or plan a dinner menu of their favorite foods on the seventh night.

Q&A FOR PARENTS

Q What should I do when my 16-year-old son refuses to practice when I'm trying to teach him a skill?

A One option is to say, "Okay." Later, when he asks you if he can do or have something, say, "I'll be glad to give you an answer after we try out that skill we talked about earlier." Also, don't always use the word "practice"; it can turn kids off. You can say something like, "Let's give it a try" or "Show me how you'd do that." Be empathetic. Tell your son you understand he might feel uncomfortable practicing at first, but that it's important for you to see that he can do the skill in a pretend situation. This will allow you to feel more comfortable about his ability to handle a real-life situation successfully on his own.

Q What if I do Preventive Teaching and my kid still misbehaves?

A For persistent misbehavior, you can use Corrective Teaching, which is explained in Chapter 10. Most kids won't learn a skill or behavior after just one practice. Teaching new skills takes time and lots of practice. Keep using Preventive Teaching and support it with Effective Praise and positive and negative consequences. Also, check to see if you need to improve on how you describe what you would like to see or whether you need to use better reasons.

Q Can I use Preventive Teaching to teach my child not to use drugs?

A Absolutely! Preventive Teaching is a great tool for discussing and teaching to this kind of issue. Preventive Teaching allows you to go over all sorts of situations with children and how to handle them. You can teach kids exactly what to say or do when they are confronted with the choice of using or not using drugs. In the end, the decision is theirs, but children are more likely to say "No" if they have been taught how and why they should do so.

Q We just did Preventive Teaching the other day before going out to eat and my child was still awful. What should I do?

A Practice, practice, practice — and then practice some more! Don't expect perfection the first time out of the blocks. Continue teaching and giving consequences and praise until your child can do what you expect in the actual situation. Preventive Teaching is no guarantee, but it makes positive behavior more likely.

Chapter 8
Reaching Goals Using Charts and Contracts

One effective way to maintain family harmony is to set up ways to keep an eye on family responsibilities by using charts and contracts. Most families have already used some method of monitoring progress in behavior. For example, Mom might keep a diet diary to monitor her eating habits while 6-year-old Danny keeps a small calendar in his dresser drawer to record his dry nights. Dad might sign a contract to cut down on smoking cigarettes, and Jennifer has a cell phone contract to pay off the text-messaging bill she ran up last month. These are all instances when a chart or contract helps parents and children meet certain goals.

Whenever you make an agreement with a child, you should spell out your expectations ahead of time. Clearly describe what the child will earn or lose when he or she behaves in certain ways. With charts and contracts, consequences are contingent on specific behaviors or social skills you want to see from your kids; for example: *"This week when you follow instructions without arguing and clean your room as soon as you get home from school, you can earn an hour to go out and play with your friends at the park across the street."* If you wrote this agreement down and signed it with your child, you would have a contract. Charts are illustrated contracts that use visual elements like stickers or stars; charts usually work best with younger children. For a middle school child, a chart could be in the form of school notes or an electronic homework journal that keeps track of school progress or grades, so the child is allowed to stay involved in extracurricular activities.

Both charts and contracts have three main points. They 1) specify the behavior or social skill your child needs to do to improve; 2) identify the privileges or possessions that can be earned or lost; and 3) indicate how long the agreement will be in effect. The goal of an agreement, whether it's a chart or contract, is to help children build their self-confidence and character by setting a reasonable goal and achieving it.

When to Use Charts and Contracts

Besides helping you keep track of how well your child is learning new skills and handling past problems, charts and contracts also show how effective your teaching is. A written agreement between you and your child allows you both to see the child's progress — no matter how small it might be. Specifically, you can use charts and contracts:

When you want to focus on a past problem behavior. For example, your child might frequently complain when asked to do something, fight with his or her siblings, or consistently be late for school in the morning.

When your child has a goal in mind. Your child may want to earn money for a new Smartphone, have later bedtimes, be allowed to use the car on weeknights, or get a job.

When you have a new goal you'd like your child to achieve. You may want your child to start a savings account, get more involved in school activities, or do his or her own laundry.

In each of these situations, a chart or a contract can be used to monitor and record the progress that is made toward the goal you or your child has in mind. Often, you can link a goal you have for your child to one he or she is anxious to achieve. For example, if your teen would like to get an after-school job, you can link that to your goal of having her complete and turn her homework assignments in on time.

Contracts

Here are three examples of how parents could use contracts to monitor their children's ability to handle more freedom, improve a morning routine, and strengthen their character by linking privileges to behaviors.

Many times, teenagers are anxious for more freedom. You can use a contract to help them prove they can handle the responsibilities that go along with increased freedom. Here's a contract parents could use with 16-year-old Tyler, who wants to drive the family car on the weekends but also needs to improve his grades in school.

Notice how Tyler's parents decided to use a calendar to help chart his progress. This will allow them to keep a daily tab on the weekly agreement. Using this kind of chart to support a contract is a good way for Tyler's parents to head off any problems.

TYLER'S CAR AGREEMENT

I, **Tyler,** agree to get my homework done on Sunday through Thursday nights by 9 p.m. In addition, each Friday, I agree to give my parents a report from my teachers that shows my progress in their classes. I have to do this each week before I can use the car on Saturday. If I am late handing in homework or a project, I will stay home on Friday and Saturday to make up the work and will not be allowed to use the car until a week after I have turned in my homework and received positive reports from my teachers.

We, **Mom and Dad,** agree to let Tyler use the family car from 8 until 11:30 p.m. on Saturday night when he completes his homework and gets positive reports from his teachers for the week.

Tyler will make a note on the family calendar each night after showing us his homework. Every Friday after we receive the written report from his teachers, we will let Tyler know he can use the car. This will continue for three months or until the contract is renegotiated.

_____   _____

(Tyler's signature)   *(Date)*

_____

(Parents' signatures)

Contracts can come in handy when parents want to improve family routines such as getting kids to follow through on after-school activities, staying on task during study time, or participating in Family Meetings. In the following example, Mom helps Rhonda work on problems with her morning routine by using her desire and motivation for phone privileges.

RHONDA'S PHONE AGREEMENT

I, **Rhonda,** will shower for no more than 10 minutes on Sunday through Friday mornings before school or church. I will start my bathroom time at 6:30 a.m. on these days. If I take longer than 10 minutes, I will lose the use of any phone until the next day. I understand if I don't set the timer before I start my shower, I won't get to use the cell phone that day.

I, **Mom,** will let Rhonda use the house or cell phone for no more than one hour each night when she is out of the bathroom on time. Rhonda must check in with me each morning before she starts her bathroom time and then again after she finishes showering and turns off the timer. We will continue this contract for two weeks.

_____   _____
(Rhonda's signature)   (Date)

_____
(Mom's signatures)

Once things are consistently better in the morning the contract can be discontinued.

Here is an example of how parents could use a contract to help a child handle a challenging situation outside the home. Kevin, 14, recently stopped helping out with the young children's Sunday School activities. At first, Kevin really liked the activities, the things he learned, the Sunday School teacher, Mr. Riggers, and the children. But now the number of children in the class has tripled, and Mr. Riggers gets frustrated when the class gets noisy and chaotic. He really needs Kevin's help, but sometimes he gets upset and yells at Kevin. After discussing things with Mr. Riggers and Kevin,

Kevin's mom and dad suggest trying a contract to help Kevin stay involved and improve his ability to stand up for himself without being rude or inappropriate.

KEVIN'S SUNDAY SCHOOL AGREEMENT

I, **Kevin,** agree to continue helping out with Sunday School activities at church. If Mr. Riggers yells and I feel upset or uncomfortable, I will politely ask him to excuse me. I will take no longer than a five-minute break if I need to calm down. Later, I will ask Mr. Riggers if I can speak with him. I will say, "Mr. Riggers, I understand things sometimes get hard, but earlier you yelled at me. It made me feel uncomfortable and scared. In the future, please talk to me without yelling at me."

I, **Mr. Riggers,** will let Kevin take a five-minute break to calm down if he feels scared or uncomfortable. Kevin will tell me in a calm voice what is bothering him and allow me to calmly respond. We will continue this contract for two weeks.

_____   _____
(Kevin's signature)   *(Date)*

_____
(Mr. Riggers' signature)

From a simple contract such as this one, Kevin can gain character-building skills like showing and earning respect, making effective decisions, and being responsible and loyal. There was no tangible reward mentioned in this contract because the positive consequences Kevin earns by fulfilling it are more natural and logical. He gets to keep doing something he likes, and he gains the respect of his teacher. Experiences like this are their own reward.

Charts

Charts are visual tools that help children work toward specific goals and show whether or not they have achieved them. They can be highly motivating, and also can make learning new skills and behaviors fun for parents and kids. Some charts are simple while others can be very elaborate, depending on the situation and the child. For example, children under the age of 8 may like more elaborate charts with moveable pieces. Let's take a look at a chart 6-year-old Bethany and her parents created. Bethany has difficulty going to bed on time, especially on weekends when both her parents are home. Her parents want Bethany to learn how to follow instructions without arguing. They decide to use a moveable chart, called "Bethany's Bedtime Steps," to help her learn to follow instructions at bedtime and go to bed on time.

To make the chart, Bethany's parents outline her footprint on five pieces of colored paper. They cut out the footprints and write a number (1 through 5) on each of the prints. On the other side of the footprints, they write a specific instruction they want Bethany to follow (brush teeth, take bath, put on pajamas, say prayer/good night, and get in bed by 8 p.m.). They then cut open a brown paper grocery bag and have Bethany trace the five footprints and write "My Goal" on the paper. On each traced footprint, Bethany's parents write a specific non-costly reward, such as Mom making a snack or Dad reading a bedtime story. The chart is then taped to Bethany's bedroom door.

Each weeknight, starting at 7:30 p.m., Bethany must follow at least three bedtime instructions (listed on the footprints) without arguing. The footprints should be located in the places where Bethany must go to get ready for bed, such as in the bathroom on the mirror or under the blankets of her bed. For each instruction she successfully follows before 8 p.m., Bethany tapes the corresponding colored footprint to the chart on her door. In addition, each night Bethany follows all five instructions and collects all five footprints, she earns 10 extra minutes to stay up on the following weekend.

While the chart described here was set up to help a child get to bed on time, it also help the child learn the social skill of "Following Instructions." Learning to follow instructions for her bedtime goal will help Bethany in similar situations where she needs to follow instructions to achieve other goals, such as completing homework, being ready for school on time in the morning, or keeping her bedroom clean.

Charts shouldn't be boring; if they are, children won't be motivated to use them. Remember, your child should be the person maintaining the chart under your supervision.

At the end of this chapter are several examples of charts you can adapt for your children. Many parents enjoy coming up with creative charts for their kids. Some of the most creative designs often come from the kids themselves. Young children, in particular, love to get out the crayons and make a colorful chart. This is a positive way to get your child involved in the process and gives you one more thing to praise.

Helpful Hints

State the goal positively.

Say, *"When you finish your homework, you can watch TV"* instead of, *"If you don't finish your homework, you can't watch TV."* Either one of these can be true, but it's easier for kids to reach a goal if they're working toward something positive.

Reinforce social skills.

When possible, use a social skill to describe the behavior you want. You could say, *"When you follow instructions and finish your homework, you can watch TV."* Linking a social skill to the behavior you want to see helps your child learn how to generalize the skill to other situations. (We will talk more about social skills and generalization in Chapter 12.)

Follow through on the agreement.

Be sure to review your child's progress each day and provide encouragement to keep going. When your child reaches the goal, deliver what you promised. And pile on the praise!

Make the goals specific and measurable.

A goal of "completing homework each night" is easier to measure than "doing better in school." Likewise, it's easier to determine if your child is "offering to help Mom once a day" than to determine if he or she is "being more responsible." Setting specific, measurable goals lets you know when your child has reached a goal.

Keep the goals reasonable.

Setting reachable goals is especially important when you are first introducing the idea of a chart or contract. When children see they can achieve a goal, they will be more motivated to work toward it.

Make it fun.

Parents use charts and contracts to help kids reach goals and experience success. This will be more enjoyable if it's fun for you and your child. Make a big deal out of each day's progress and use lots of praise during the day when your child is working toward the goal.

Summary

Charts and contracts are a great way to help your children set goals and see the successes they achieve. Charts and contracts also open up lines of communication between you and your children and help you reach goals together. Identifying goals and planning how to reach them requires conversation and negotiation between you and your child. The time you spend with your children setting up charts or contracts shows them you care and are interested in helping them succeed.

Before kids get to do what they want, they have to keep their end of the bargain. Charts and contracts are simple, straightforward, and geared toward helping parents and children make improvements and get things accomplished.

HEATHER'S HOMEWORK HELPER

1. Start homework immediately after dinner.

2. Ask Mom to check homework.

3. Finish homework by 8:30 p.m.

4. Read for 20 minutes.

Each day all four stars are filled in, I may choose one of the following:

- 45 minutes of telephone time
- 45 minutes of watching TV
- 45 minutes of computer time

Reggie's Rebound

Each day I finish my chore of feeding the dog, I get to color a basketball. Every day I color a ball, I get to shoot baskets outside with Dad for 15 minutes.

End of the Week Bonus

On Saturday, I get a bonus for having 4 or more balls colored during the week.

4 balls colored = watch a movie on Saturday
5 balls colored = friends come over on Saturday
6 balls colored = bike ride on Sunday with Dad
7 balls colored = friends stay overnight on Saturday

Tiffany's Four-Star Behavior Chart

	Get along with brother and sister	Give Mom and Dad a smile and hug before and after school	Be polite to Mom and Dad	Get ready for and be in bed by 9 p.m.
SUN				
SAT				
FRI				
THURS				
WED				
TUES				
MON				

☆ ☆ ☆

Each day that I have **3 stars**, I get to pick one of the following:

1. Call a friend on the phone.
2. Ride my bike.
3. Play a game of my choice with Mom or Dad.

☆ ☆ ☆ ☆

Each day that I have **4 stars**, I get to pick two from this list or the 3-star list.

1. Go to bed 15 minutes later.
2. Use the computer for 30 minutes.
3. Watch TV for 30 minutes.

Jamar's Chore Calendar

	Make Bed	Empty waste baskets	Clear dishes from dinner table	Put dirty clothes in hamper
SUN				
SAT				
FRI				
THURS				
WED				
TUES				
MON				

☆ ☆ ☆ ☆

I can earn **4 stickers** each day. The number of stickers I have on my chart tells me what special things I get to do each day.

1 Sticker   =   Get snack after school.
2 Stickers =   Get snack and take a bike ride.
3 Stickers =   Get snack, take bike ride, and 30 minutes of video game time.
4 Stickers =   Get all of above and go to bed 15 minutes later then usual.

☞ CHAPTER REVIEW

What is the goal of using charts and contracts?

To monitor and change children's behavior.

When should charts and contracts be used?

When you want to focus on a past problem behavior, when your child has a goal in mind, and when you have a goal you want to see your child achieve.

☆ ACTION PLAN

1 Take some time to answer the following questions:
- What is the most important thing you learned in this chapter?
- What do you plan to do differently as a result of what you learned?

2. Choose a problem behavior you would like to see your child improve on. If your child is a teen, sit down with him or her and write a contract that promises a reward for improving that behavior. Be specific in describing the improvements you want to see. Ask your child what privilege he or she would like as a reward if the behavior does improve. Write the reward into the contract.

If your child is younger, create a chart (based on one of the samples provided in this chapter) listing the positive behaviors you want to see. Discuss with your child the reward(s) he or she would like to receive for meeting the behavior goals. Post the chart in a highly visible spot (refrigerator or bedroom door). Provide colorful markers or stickers your child can use to mark his or her progress on the chart each day.

Correcting Problem Behavior

In our experience, the number one reason parents seek help with their children is dealing with misbehavior. Misbehavior is a fact of life for any parent; kids are going to cry, argue, resist, not follow instructions, and even get so angry they lash out when things don't go their way. Parents must remember this doesn't mean their children are bad or mean, or they are bad parents who are failing their children. Most kids misbehave because they are not motivated to learn positive behaviors or because they are not skilled enough to correct their negative behaviors.

Oftentimes, children misbehave as a way to get attention. For many, getting attention for bad behavior is better than getting no attention at all. Other kids let their emotions get the best of them, acting out before they think about how their behavior will affect them and the people around them. Many young children (and even some older ones) have not reached a maturity level where they can control their emotions and refrain from using negative behavior. Parents must look at misbehavior as an opportunity to teach children a new way of behaving.

The first key to dealing with children's misbehavior is staying calm. Nothing gets accomplished if you are yelling as loudly as your child or displaying the very behaviors you are trying to stop. These types of situations only lead to hurt feelings and bad relationships between parents and children. When parents lose control of their emotions, they also send a message to children that the way to handle a problem is to scream, yell, and lose control.

In this section, we will first discuss how you can stay calm when dealing with any kind of misbehavior from your children, whether it is as minor as running through the house or as severe as a full-blown temper tantrum. Then we will provide two valuable parenting skills that will help you navigate through the often-frustrating situations when your children aren't doing what they're supposed to do, doing something they shouldn't, or doing something that could be harmful to themselves or others.

The first skill you will learn is called **Corrective Teaching**, which can be used for a wide range of children's negative behaviors. The second skill, **Teaching Self-Control**, is used in situations where it has become impossible for a parent to continue to teach a child because the child is no longer responding to Corrective Teaching, or because his or her behavior has worsened or become too disruptive. This could involve a child totally losing emotional control or "shutting down" and refusing to talk or respond.

Successful outcomes depend on you knowing whether Corrective Teaching has accomplished the goal of stopping your child's negative behavior or whether you must move to

Teaching Self-Control. Sometimes, children are willing to be corrected; they misbehave, and you are able to address the behavior using Corrective Teaching. But when kids are so upset they can't calm down, you will need to use Teaching Self-Control.

It is equally important that you continue to teach and help your children practice alternative positive behaviors after a problem behavior has stopped or after a child has regained self-control. And in any teaching situation, you should remain calm and keep your child's safety as your first priority, no matter what he or she says or does. Some parents think that because a child is out of control, they have a right to lose their temper, too. But you must remember you can control only your own behavior. You must remain calm and focus on what you are trying to teach your child by setting your own positive example.

Chapter 9
Staying Calm

M any parents find the biggest challenge they face in dealing with their child's problem behaviors is staying calm themselves. We all know there are times when our kids are going to make us upset and angry. Children can be sarcastic, defiant, rebellious, and sometimes even violent. You can prepare yourself for times like these by learning to keep your cool.

Please understand we are not saying you won't get angry. That's impossible, maybe even unhealthy, since anger is a basic human emotion. Blowing your top over your child's behavior, however, can make these situations worse. We point out to parents that "anger" is just one letter away from "danger."

When parents describe what they do when they are angry, they typically admit to yelling, swearing, or threatening their children. Some say they hit, throw, or kick things. Many parents are convinced these angry responses work because they show children they "mean business." In a certain respect, they are right. These angry responses do often stop the problem behavior, at least temporarily. But what do children really learn from such parental behavior? They learn to yell, hit, and throw or kick things when they are upset.

When parents go through our Common Sense Parenting classes, one of the most important things they learn is how to stay calm in explosive situations. And when they do, they report the following results:

1. Their kids' temper tantrums or problem behaviors stop sooner.

2. The problem behaviors aren't as severe.

3. The parents feel better about the way they handled a situation.

One stepparent told us, "You know, that 'calm' thing really works. My son used to run away frequently. Usually, it was after he did something wrong and I'd get mad at him. Then we'd start arguing and he'd leave. After I learned how to stay calm and not go bonkers, we both stayed calmer and were able to work things out without him running away."

Of course, staying calm was just one of the effective changes this dad made in his parenting style. As he learned to remain calm, he was able to put his other parenting skills to work. This led to a dramatic, positive change in his relationship with his stepson.

Planning ahead is important to remaining calm. If you wait until you're in the middle of an emotional situation to figure out ways to calm down, you're unlikely to be successful. Creating a "Staying Calm Plan" is a good way to develop and practice effective strategies for keeping your cool. There are four steps to developing your Staying Calm Plan:

1. Identify **what your children say and do** that makes you angry.

2. Recognize the signs (**how you feel and what you do**) that indicate you are getting upset.

3. Decide **what you could do differently** to stay calm in the future.

4. Make a **Staying Calm Plan** that will work for you.

Step One: What Makes You Angry?

Knowing what makes us angry is the first step in being able to respond calmly to our children's problem behaviors. Typically, kids are able to push our buttons — say the words or do the things that get under our skin. When we ask parents what upsets them most, they often respond with, *"I hate it when he talks back to me,"* or *"Her moodiness drives me crazy!"* What is more helpful than these general statements is for parents to describe the specific behaviors that irritate and upset them. For example, they should say, *"When I ask my son to empty the trash cans, he says things like, 'Where's the fire? They'll still be there tomorrow,'"* or *"When I ask my daughter how her day at school went, she sulks and refuses to answer me."* If parents can identify in advance the behaviors that trigger their anger, they'll be better able to reduce the intensity and severity of their own response to those behaviors.

On a piece of paper, draw four columns. At the top of the first column, write the words, "My child's problem behaviors." In that column, list the specific problem behaviors your kids do that really bother or upset you. Make sure you specifically describe what your kids say, what they do, and what voice tone they use. Also, include where and when a behavior usually happens. Does it occur after you give them an instruction, correct a misbehavior, or ask them to help around the house? Or does it happen at a certain time of day, such as after school or right before bedtime? The more specific you make your list, the more likely you will be to recognize similar situations in their early stages in the future.

At the top of the three remaining columns, write the following headings: "Annoyed," "Angry," and "Blow my top." Then, across from each behavior you described and listed in the first column, put a check mark in the column that best describes the level of anger you feel when your child does that particular behavior. This exercise will help you recognize the situations and behaviors you most need to focus on when building your Staying Calm Plan.

Step Two: What Are Your Warning Signs?

There are a whole series of biological changes and emotions that flood our bodies when we start to get upset. As a result, our behavior often changes dramatically. Identifying these "red flags" allows us to think before we act. It's much easier to remain calm when we recognize these "red flags" early on, before our anger jumps to higher levels.

What are your "red flags"? Does your heart race or your face get flushed? Do you clench your teeth, make a fist, or feel your muscles tighten? Do you talk faster or louder or start pointing and making rude or hurtful statements? Do you begin feeling anxious, frustrated, or even ill? Take some time to think about the earliest warning signs that indicate you're beginning to get upset. On the back of the sheet of paper where you listed your children's behaviors and your anger levels, write down the things you feel or do when you're beginning to get angry or annoyed. These will be the earliest warning signals that tell you it's time to calm down.

Identifying your "red flags" as early as possible is a key to successfully staying calm.

Step Three: What Can You Do to Stay Calm?

Next, think of two or three things you could do that would help you stay calm. Consider things you can do or say that are immediate and that don't require support from anyone or anything. For example, you might take deep breaths, count to 10, or go to a quiet spot to cool down and think. Some people may need to distance themselves from the situation for a bit or blow off steam by doing something that is physically or mentally distracting. Activities like vacuuming, doing a crossword puzzle, taking a walk, listening to music, and others can be helpful. Here are some other things parents do to calm down in upsetting situations:

- *"I count to 10 — very slowly. I concentrate on doing that regardless of what my son is yelling."*
- *"I put my hands in my pockets. I tend to talk with my hands, especially when I'm angry. Before I learned to do this, I think my daughter thought I was going to hit her. I wasn't, but she viewed my behavior as a threat."*
- *"I pray, meditate, or read scripture. I ask God for strength to stay calm."*
- *"I sit down. If I'm standing, I begin to tremble. Sitting calms me for some reason. I can still tell my child what he's doing wrong, but I say it a lot more calmly."*
- *"I take a deep breath and let it out slowly a few times. This kind of serves as a safety valve to me. It's like I'm letting steam out of my body."*

- *"I just leave the situation for a while. I go to another room until I can handle myself. I figure if my kid's that mad, taking a little time to regain my control won't hurt anything. I can deal with it a lot better that way. Sometimes, he even calms down by the time I get back."*

- *"This may sound crazy, but I wear a rubber band on my wrist and snap the band whenever I feel like I'm getting upset. That's a signal to myself I'd better calm down."*

- *"I used to get so upset with my 15-year-old, I would have to go outside for a walk to calm down. I couldn't do this every time, but it's been helpful on many occasions."*

- *"I call someone like my best friend or my sister. By talking about the situation, I can go back in and deal with it more calmly."*

- *"I sit down and on paper write about how upset I am. Sometimes, I can't even read what I've written. That's not as important as the fact I'm not taking it out on my son. When I calm down, I'm always surprised at how upset I got over such a little thing."*

Now it's time for you to make a list of three different strategies you want to use to calm down, depending on whether you are annoyed, angry, or ready to blow your top. You might want to combine some strategies for the best possible result; for example, "I'll count to 10 while I rinse my face with cool water." These calming methods, along with the previous lists you made, will give you the necessary information for creating your own Staying Calm Plan.

Step Four: Make a Staying Calm Plan That Will Work for You

Now, let's put together all the information you gathered from the previous steps. That means combining:

1. What your child does that makes you upset

2. The early warning signals that tell you you're getting annoyed

3. A way of staying calm that works for you

On a new sheet of paper, write a Staying Calm Plan for yourself. Parents tell us that when they write down their plan, they are more likely to remember it and use it during a confrontation with their child. Your plan should follow this outline:

The next time my child *(child's problem behavior),* **and I start** *(early warning signals),* **I will** *(what I will do to stay calm).*

The following is an example of one mother's Staying Calm Plan:

"The next time Johnny talks back to me and refuses to go to bed, and I start feeling my heart pound, I will take three deep breaths and let them out slowly before I correct him."

Staying calm wasn't easy for this parent at first. She had to work at it. But the more she concentrated on and practiced her plan, the more successful she was at staying calm. She said she felt better about the way she interacted with her son and felt a sense of pride in maintaining her self-control. Once you have written down your plan, practice what you will do the next time your child's behavior sparks your anger.

Tips for Staying Calm

Learning to control your negative reactions will take some time. Don't get discouraged if you lose your temper every now and then. Here are some tips that have helped other parents:

Practice positive thinking.

Negative, self-defeating thoughts lead to more problems. If you find yourself thinking negative thoughts, interrupt them by saying "Stop it!" to yourself. Then refocus with positive thoughts. Here are some examples:

- *"Relax. Take it easy."*
- *"I am going to help my child."*
- *"Take it slowly."*
- *"I'm a good parent and I can do this."*
- *"It's going to get better. It just takes time."*

You will find the more often you use positive thinking, the better you will feel about yourself and your role as a parent. Even if you don't see any immediate change in your child's behavior, you can certainly prevent the problem from getting worse. By thinking positive thoughts, you not only learn to control your emotions but also are able to concentrate on the task at hand — teaching your children better ways to behave.

Don't take what your child says personally.

This may be very difficult when your child is calling you every name in the book. You must convince yourself this is happening because your child hasn't yet acquired the necessary skills for dealing with his or her own anger or frustration. Don't react when your child calls you a name or accuses you of being a rotten parent. When you can let negative, angry comments bounce off you, your teaching will be more effective. If you are concerned about something your child says, use a problem-solving approach after he or she has calmed down.

"Take five."

Instead of blurting out an angry response, take five minutes to think about what is happening and how you should respond. It is remarkable how this "cooling off" period can help you regain self-control and put things in perspective. Simply leaving the situation sometimes can help to defuse a volatile confrontation.

Focus on actual behavior rather than what you think are the reasons for your child's misbehavior.

Don't look for motives; instead, deal with the way your child is acting. You can drive yourself batty trying to figure out reasons for your child's negative behavior. After the problem is solved, take the time to talk to your child about what happened and why.

If you get angry and say or do something you regret, go back and say you're sorry.

Apologize, say what you did wrong, and tell your child what you're going to do differently next time. This models for your children what they should do when they make a mistake. Some parents worry about apologizing to their kids because they think it means they're losing some of their parental authority. But apologizing helps kids realize we all, young and old, make mistakes. Admitting a mistake is the responsible thing to do. It's best to apologize and do your best not to let it happen again.

Staying calm does not mean being totally passive.

There are times when it is appropriate to raise your voice — but you should use a firm, no-nonsense voice tone that's not too loud or overly emotional. You can be emphatic, but only if what you say is a specific description of your child's behavior and not a judgment, putdown, or expression of negative feelings.

The Safe Home Plan

When they are upset, some children can become aggressive or even violent. They may take their anger out on everyone, or their behavior may get so out of control they make the home unsafe for others, especially siblings. In special cases like these, parents should teach their children safe ways to respond when a sibling is out of control.

Here are some suggestions you can use to develop your own Safe Home Plan:

1. **Parents should discuss and decide on details of the plan ahead of time.** Decide what problem behaviors could lead to your putting the Safe Home Plan into effect (for example, children threatening to harm themselves, threats to harm others, destroying objects, etc.).

Identify specific behaviors other children in the home should or should not use when the plan is put into action (for example, do leave the room, don't join in the argument). Agree on positive and negative consequences you will use when your children follow or don't follow the plan.

2. **Talk with your children at a Family Meeting** (covered in Chapter 14) about the Safe Home Plan before using it or making it an official family plan.

3. **Write down key points about how the plan will work** and post the list in a place where everyone can see it and follow the plan when the time comes. (Try not to overuse or underuse the plan; these kinds of extremes make the plan less effective.)

An example of a Safe Home Plan might be:

Whenever we think a family member's behavior is getting so out of control it might be dangerous to the person or others in the family, the Safe Home Plan will be put into action. You should immediately go to the designated safe place in the house (your bedroom) or leave the house with Mom or Dad, if necessary. Once things calm down, one of us will call off the Safe Home Plan. Everyone who obeys the plan will earn (list the positive consequence). Everyone who does not obey the plan will earn (list the negative consequence).

Summary

It's not always easy to stay calm when you're dealing with children's negative behavior. But parents report it's one of the most important keys to effective parenting. If you can stay calm, you'll find it easier to teach your kids positive ways of handling problems. Identify what your child does that makes you angry. Look at your own early warning signals that tell you when you're getting upset. Then develop a plan for staying calm. Finally, use your plan for staying calm to help you deal with emotionally intense situations with your children.

⤳ CHAPTER REVIEW

What are the steps to creating a Staying Calm Plan?

1. Identify what your children say and do that makes you angry.
2. Recognize the signs (how you feel and what you do) that indicate you are getting upset.
3. Decide what you could do differently to stay calm in the future.
4. Make a Staying Calm Plan that will work for you.

Why is it important to stay calm?

Parents can avoid damaging their relationship with their children and be more effective in addressing their behaviors and teaching skills.

When should you use a Safe Home Plan?

When children are threatening to harm themselves, threatening to harm others, or damaging or destroying property.

☆ ACTION PLAN

1. Take some time to answer the following questions:
   - What is the most important thing you learned in this chapter?
   - What do you plan to do differently as a result of what you learned?

2. Select one behavior your child does that upsets you. Write down a Staying Calm Plan for it and practice the plan for a week. If your calming down strategy doesn't work well for you, choose and practice a different one. The following week, add another problem behavior to the plan and practice for that behavior.

Q&A
FOR PARENTS

Q **What should I do when more than one child is misbehaving and they gang up on me?"**

A Use the same Staying Calm Plan. Also, use your Safe Home Plan sooner to separate the children, before they start feeding on each other's negative behavior. When children "gang up" on parents, it's time for parents to start doing more proactive teaching and less reactive teaching. Once things calm down, have your children spend a lot of time with you practicing how to calm down, reviewing the Safe Home Plan, developing a Staying Calm Plan for themselves, and working off the significant negative consequence they will have earned for their behavior.

Q **How can I correct my children for yelling at each other when my spouse yells at them?**

A Talk to your spouse about how you both must make a conscious effort to model good communication skills for your children. Changing old habits is difficult, and sometimes you'll make mistakes. So, set up a "reminder phrase" for you and your spouse to use when one or the other starts yelling, something you've both agreed on ahead of time; for example, "Honey, the biscuits are burning." The phrase should remind whichever spouse is yelling to use his or her Staying Calm Plan. After he or she has cooled down, that parent should apologize to everyone and calmly deal with the children's behavior. Becoming a calmer parent won't happen overnight. But if you and your spouse support each other and really work at it, you and your children will see improvement.

CHAPTER 10
Correcting Misbehavior

"No, I don't want to go to bed!"

"The teacher's lying. I did my homework!"

"Mom... he hit me!"

ound familiar? Children constantly test limits. In many respects, this is healthy. Testing limits is one way children grow and learn about the world around them. However, when kids continually test limits and misbehave, parents can lose patience and question their ability to deal with their children's difficult behavior. Constant misbehavior and the parental anger and frustration that result from it can make for a very stressful and unhappy home. That's why many parents in our Common Sense Parenting classes can't wait for us to talk about how to stop children's problem behavior. In this chapter, we will discuss **Corrective Teaching, a parenting technique that stops misbehavior, delivers a consequence, and teaches children a positive, alternative way of behaving.**

It's important to point out that correcting negative behavior should be only one part of your approach to effective parenting. While you learn the steps of Corrective Teaching, remember you also must teach your expectations to your children ahead of time using Preventive Teaching so they know what you want. And, you must build positive relationships with your children through Effective Praise so they're more willing to cooperate with you in times of stress. Parents who don't use these two parenting tools often will generally have a difficult time effectively correcting their children when they misbehave.

Parents usually have no problem listing the kinds of negative behavior that frustrates them. There's a good chance some of the following complaints we've heard also apply to your family:

- *"I always have to ask two or three times whenever I want my children to do something."*

- *"It seems like my kids fight all the time. They just pick, pick, pick at one another until one of them gets mad."*

- *"My son does nothing but play video games. He won't do his homework. He doesn't help out. He just sits in front of that screen."*

- *"I can't get my children to do anything around the house unless I threaten to take away privileges."*

- *"When I ask my son about his homework, he says it's done or he left it at school. Sooner or later, I get a note from the teacher."*

- *"I'm so tired of my kids arguing or whining every time I ask them to do something. It just wears me out."*

- *"My daughter sneaks money out of my purse and then lies about it when I confront her."*

These parents, like most concerned parents, are looking for a constructive, effective way to respond to their children's problem behavior. The five-step process of Corrective Teaching helped these parents, and it can help you too.

When to Use Corrective Teaching

When correcting your child's misbehaviors, it is best to pick your battles. Sometimes when your child tests your limits, you might only use a firm instruction, small consequences, or redirection to correct his or her misbehavior. Redirection is simply using gentle physical guidance or a verbal instruction that moves a child's point of interest away from a negative behavior and toward an appropriate behavior. For example, if your young child is whining about a long car ride, you might give him a toy to play with or play a game with him to redirect his attention away from what he is complaining about.

On the other hand, **when children frequently do things they shouldn't do, or don't do things they should do, or engage in unsafe behavior, it is time to use Corrective Teaching.** If you limit using Corrective Teaching to the times when your child exhibits severe or persistent defiant behavior, you can avoid overusing or underusing this skill.

Deciding whether or not a situation warrants using Corrective Teaching is a skill you must master if your teaching is to be effective. Look at the examples below and decide whether you could correct the problem behavior with a simple instruction, prompt, consequence, or redirection, or if the more serious intervention of Corrective

Teaching is needed.

1. Every Friday, your teenager forgets to do his regular chore of taking out the trash before the trash collectors arrive.

2. You find your 8-year-old playing with matches in his closet.

3. For the third time in a week, your daughter dresses for school in a revealing outfit and argues with you when you tell her to change out of it.

4. You tell your 15-year-old son he can't attend a party tonight, and he storms out of the house and doesn't come back until midnight.

5. Your 6-year-old twins blame each other when you ask who broke their new toy.

6. Your daughter usually puts gas in the car when she goes out with her friends, but today the fuel gauge is on empty when you get in the car to go to work.

7. Your 10-year-old accidentally drops an entire gallon of milk on the floor.

Of these seven situations, the first four are good examples of times when you should use Corrective Teaching because they involve negative behaviors that are either serious or frequently test your limits. The last three situations involve accidental, infrequent, or minor misbehaviors you could try to address using a small consequence or a firm instruction. Of course, every parent has his or her own limits and expectations. You can choose to use Corrective Teaching to stop and address any problem behavior.

The Steps of Corrective Teaching

One parent told us, *"Corrective Teaching gives me a plan that lays out how and what to teach my kids when they misbehave. I was doing some of it sometimes — like giving consequences — but I really wasn't teaching. So my kids never learned what they should do. They only heard what I didn't like."*

As this parent discovered, Corrective Teaching combines clear messages with consequences and practicing appropriate skills to help parents respond to problem behavior. When it is used to address frequent limit-testing behaviors, Corrective Teaching gives you a complete package of effective and simple steps for responding to misbehaviors and teaching children desired alternative behaviors.

The first step of Corrective Teaching is describing the problem behavior to the child and firmly telling him or her to stop it. The parent then gives the child a negative consequence, either the loss of a privilege or the addition of a chore. Next, the parent describes the desired behavior the child should use instead of the misbehavior and explains why the desired behavior should be used. Finally, the parent has the child practice the desired behavior. This final step assures the parent that the child understands and can perform the desired behavior. Here are those steps again:

1. Stop/Describe the problem behavior.
2. Give a negative consequence (loss of privilege or added chore).
3. Describe the desired behavior.
4. Give a reason
5. Practice.

Let's look at an example of Corrective Teaching: You come home from work and your daughter has a bunch of kids in the house who are loud and rowdy. She didn't call to ask you if it was okay to have her friends over after school. You tell your daughter the party's over and it's time for her to tell her friends to leave. She argues with you, calling you unfair, saying her friends weren't doing anything wrong. Using a firm but calm voice tone, you tell her to follow you to the kitchen or bedroom. Giving this instruction helps you see if she is open to your correction. It also removes her from distractions and the motivation to be defiant in front of her friends. Once you and your daughter are alone, you can begin the steps to Corrective Teaching. Here's what your teaching might sound like:

1. **Stop/Describe the problem behavior.**

    Mom: *"Stephanie, you are **arguing and making excuses** because I told you to ask your friends to leave. **Please stop.**"* (Stephanie stops arguing.)

2. **Give a negative consequence.**

    Mom: *"Because you argued and didn't follow my instructions, **you can't use your cell phone tonight.**"*

3. **Describe the desired behavior.**

    Mom: *"I know you like having your friends over, but when I give you an instruction, I want you to **look at me, say 'Okay,' and then do what I ask. If you disagree,** remember to **calm down** before you try to discuss it with me. Okay?"*

4. Give a reason.

Mom: *"It's important to follow in-structions **because I am more likely to listen to you."***

5. Practice.

Mom: *"Now, let's practice this. I am going to give you an instruction, and you follow it by telling your friends it's time to go home. How are you going to follow instructions the next time I ask you to tell your friends it's time to go home?"*

Stephanie: **"I'll look at you, say 'Okay,' and then tell my friends they have to go home."**

Mom: *"Great! What if you start to get angry?"*

Stephanie: **"Well, I should try to stay calm and wait until I cool down to discuss it with you."**

Mom: *"Exactly! When you're calm, cool, and collected, I'm more likely to listen to you. **Let's see if you can follow this next instruction.** I want you to ask your friends to leave, clean up the mess you made in the family room, and then help me start dinner."* (Stephanie says *"Okay,"* and heads to the family room.)

Of course, things might not go this smoothly every time you use Corrective Teaching, but this example gives you a picture of how the steps should be used. If your child starts trying to sidetrack you by debating or arguing, you should simply say, *"We're not talking about that right now. Let's focus on your behavior."* Or just ignore the arguing and continue correcting the child.

If your child starts yelling or refuses to do what you ask, or if the child's behavior gets worse in other ways, it's time to move to another parenting skill called **Teaching Self-Control**. This skill gives you a way to respond to emotionally intense situations with your children. (We will discuss Teaching Self-Control in the next chapter.)

Here's a brief explanation of each of the Corrective Teaching steps:

STEP 1: Stop/Describe the Problem Behavior

Stopping the problem behavior as soon as it starts is easier than waiting until the behavior goes on for a long time or escalates. Waiting to correct it also might give your child the false impression the misbehavior is okay or not important to you. Start with praise and empathy, then calmly get the child's attention, describe the problem behavior, and give him or her a clear instruction such as, *"Jason, I know you're upset, but stop yelling at and pushing your brother. Please come over here and sit down in this chair."* Eliminate as many distractions as possible and get at the child's eye level. This will help the child concentrate on you and your teaching. Once the problem behavior has stopped, specifically describe it. For example, a mom might say, *"Rachel, please come over here so I can talk with you.* (Rachel walks over to her mother.) *I know you wanted to just relax, but before I left for the store, I asked you to pick up your clothes and put away the clean dishes. Your clothes are still on the floor, the dishes aren't put away, and it looks like you've been lying on the couch, listening to music instead."*

STEP 2: Give a Negative Consequence

Consequences help children make the connection between what they do and what happens as a result of their actions. Negative consequences, such as removing a privilege or adding a chore, reduce the frequency and/or severity of the behaviors they follow. In other words, if Mom wants Rachel to follow instructions right away, she would say, *"Since you didn't do what I asked, you can fold all the laundry after you pick up your clothes and put away the dishes. All this has to be done before you turn your music on again."*

You can use one or a combination of small consequences to encourage children to change their behavior. If the problem behavior is significant and requires a large consequence, prepare your child and offer him or her the chance to earn some of the privilege back; for example, *"When you're able to accept a consequence, it's more likely you will be able to earn back some of the privileges you lost."* When you choose consequences, remember the characteristics that make them effective: importance, immediacy, frequency, size, and contingency.

The next two steps are extremely important because they help parents focus on teaching children a desired behavior they can use instead of what they did wrong.

STEP 3: Describe the Desired Behavior

This is similar to the step you used in Effective Praise and Preventive Teaching. Label the skill, be clear and specific, and stick to describing what desired behavior you want your child to use in place of the problem behavior. (Use the skills described in Chapter 12 to help you identify what you want your child to do instead of the misbehavior.) In our example, Rachel didn't follow her mom's instructions to do a couple of chores. Her mom might say, *"Rachel, any time I give you an instruction, I want you to say 'Okay' and get started on it right away."*

STEP 4: Give a Reason

Giving a reason helps to explain to a child the importance of using a skill or behavior. During Corrective Teaching, giving a reason can also help the child connect the behavior to the consequence or the outcome; for example, *"Now, you'll finish your chores sooner and be able to get back to your music."*

STEP 5: Practice

Each time your children practice doing things right, you are increasing their chances for success and decreasing the likelihood you will see the problem behavior in the future. By practicing, you give them one more opportunity to learn something new. Practice helps them remember just what they can do to avoid problems and get things right. For example, Mom might say, *"Rachel, show me how you're going to follow instructions and get your chores done next time."* And Rachel might slowly answer, *"All right,"* and walk off to get started on her chores. A little later, Mom can tell Rachel, *"Thanks for getting started right away."*

Examples of Corrective Teaching

Here are some more examples of Corrective Teaching:

A father tells his son he's grounded from going out with friends or driving the car for the next two weeks because he was suspended from school for starting a fight.

1. Stop/Describe the problem behavior.

Dad: *"Mark, please listen and look at me.*

(Mark looks at his father.)

Thank you. I know things can get tough at school but fighting never solves anything."

2. Give a negative consequence.

Dad: *"Since you weren't respectful of others, you will not be allowed to go out with your friends or drive your car for two weeks. Also, you will need to apologize to the boys you got in a fight with when you return to school."*

3. Describe the desired behavior.

Dad: *"When you have a disagreement with someone and things start getting out of control, remember to stay calm by taking a few deep breaths, count to yourself, or just get away from the situation."*

4. Give a reason.

Dad: *"Remember, if you stay calm, you won't make the situation worse for yourself."*

5. Practice

Dad: *"Now, here's a chance for you to show me you know how to stay calm. You've done a great job of listening so far. Let's practice what you would do or say*

> *if you were trying to get your home-*
> *work done tonight and your brother*
> *interrupts and starts teasing you?"*

Mark: (sighs)

> *"I would take a deep breath, count*
> *to ten, or get away from him for a*
> *while so I could calm down."*

Dad: *"Good. That's right."*

Two young sisters are fighting over a toy while their father is on an important telephone call. Dad excuses himself from the call and sits down to get at eye level with his daughters.

1. Stop/Describe the problem behavior.

Dad: *"Jamie and Alisha, please come here*
> *and sit on the couch. I know you both*
> *want the toy, but while I was talking on*
> *the phone, you two were fighting and*
> *screaming over it and not sharing."*

Jamie: *"But Daddy, she started it!"*

Dad: *"Jamie, we're not talking about who*
> *started the fight. Let's focus on you*
> *two not sharing."*

2. Give a negative consequence.

Dad: *"Because you weren't sharing, you*
> *both have to sit here in Time-Out*
> *for six minutes."* (With young chil-
> dren, it is probably more effective to
> have them first sit in Time-Out for
> the required time and then tell them
> what to do in future situations.)

3. Describe the desired behavior.

Dad: *"I want you two to learn how to share better. Alisha, when your sister wants a toy you have but you're not finished playing with it, tell her, 'Okay. I'll be done in five minutes.' Then set the timer. Jamie, if you ask for a toy and your sister says, 'No, I just started playing with it,' just say 'Okay' and find another toy to play with until she is finished. If you still need help, quietly come and get me. Okay?"*

4. Give a reason.

Dad:: *"When you share, you both are more likely to have fun playing with the toy."*

5. Practice.

Dad: (talking to both daughters) *"Let's pretend one of you is playing with a toy and the other asks if she can play with it. Let's practice. What can you say?"*

Alisha: *"Can I have a turn playing with that when you're done?"*

Dad: *"All right! That's a great way to ask. Now Jamie, what would you say to your sister?"*

Jamie: *"I'll be done in five minutes."*

Dad: *"Good! Remember to set the timer and come get me if there are any problems. Okay? Good job, girls, with practicing how to share!"*

Helpful Hints

Remain calm.

This is easy to say, but not always easy to do. If misbehavior happens often or the behavior itself is very annoying, you may find it difficult to keep your temper in check. However, parents consistently tell us this is the most crucial thing you can do when using Corrective Teaching. By staying calm, you decrease the chances your child will get upset or escalate the misbehavior.

Stick to one issue.

Most children are masters at getting their parents sidetracked. Some can get parents so far off the topic they forget what the original issue was. Familiar lines like these can be particularly effective at redirecting parents' attention:

- *"You hate me! Don't you?"*
- *"My friends don't have to do that. Why are you so hard on me?"*
- *"I don't want to talk about it. And you can't make me!"*
- *"You can take away anything you want. I just don't care."*
- *"I want to go and live with Dad. He really loves me!"*

Comments like these can hurt us or tempt us to respond sarcastically. Or, you might feel like listing all the good things you do for your child. It's best, however, to resist responding to provocative comments or side issues. Stick with what you want to teach. If your child really wants to talk about other topics, he or she can bring them up after the main issue (the misbehavior) is resolved.

Provide a chance to earn back part of a privilege.

If your child is attentive, accepts responsibility for the misbehavior, and works hard to make up for what he or she did wrong, and you are pleased with the attempt, allow the child to earn back part of the privilege you took away. This is called **positive correction.** Here's how it works: During Corrective Teaching, your son and daughter lose one hour of TV time because they were arguing. After you finish your teaching, both children apologize and work together to get their evening chores done. If they cooperate and complete the chore, they can earn back up to half of the TV time they lost. Doing this allows you to give them a positive consequence for working on the skill of getting along with each other. Positive correction is an effective way to teach children how to make up for mistakes or misbehaviors.

Be consistent.

Knowing what to expect from you helps your children feel secure and encourages them to behave well. If you set a bedtime for your children, you need to consistently correct them and give consequences when they miss it, and praise them when they are in bed on time. Be sure to use Effective Praise and maybe even some creative rewards when they meet your expectations. When a child misbehaves or breaks an important family rule, use Corrective Teaching consistently to teach your child you mean what you say.

Be flexible.

While you should consistently use Corrective Teaching for misbehavior, you can be flexible in the way you use it.

No one knows your child better than you. If your daughter gets too upset if you give her a consequence right after stopping a negative behavior, put the consequence at the end of the teaching sequence when she's likely to be calmer.

Use consequences.

Some parents feel uncomfortable using consequences, even as the last step in the teaching sequence. Some behaviors may change when parents use Corrective Teaching without the "consequence" step because the time the parent spends teaching the child is enough of a consequence. But using consequences will usually increase the effectiveness of teaching because children are more likely to make the connection between what they did and what they get to do or don't get to do. They realize quickly that by stopping negative behavior, they also can avoid losing privileges and gaining extra chores.

Summary

Parents who take the time to use each of the steps of Corrective Teaching will find it helps to change problem behaviors. Children learn that misbehavior brings consequences. At the same time, your teaching is helping them learn new and better behaviors to replace those that get them into trouble. If you are consistent, children eventually will understand what your tolerances are and won't test your limits as often. Coupled with Preventive Teaching and Effective Praise, Corrective Teaching can greatly reduce the amount of misbehavior you will have to deal with and make your home a far more pleasant and positive place for you and your children.

🐦 CHAPTER REVIEW

What are the five steps of Corrective Teaching?

1. Stop/Describe the problem behavior.
2. Give a negative consequence.
3. Describe the desired behavior.
4. Give a reason.
5. Practice.

When should parents use Corrective Teaching?

1. When children aren't doing what they should be doing.
2. When children are doing something they shouldn't be doing.
3. When children are doing something unsafe.

What is positive correction?

Positive correction is allowing a child to earn back some of the privileges he or she has lost, as long as the following criteria are met: The child is attentive, accepts responsibility for the misbehavior, and works hard to make up for what he or she did wrong, and you are pleased with the attempt.

✩ ACTION PLAN

1. Take some time to answer the following questions:
   - What is the most important thing you learned in this chapter?

- What do you plan to do differently as a result of what you've learned?

2. Think about one of your child's typical misbehaviors. Figure out what you would say for each Corrective Teaching step to address the behavior. Practice the steps in front of a mirror a few times before using it with your child. Mirrors are a friendly place to start; they don't talk back as much as children. Once you've seen and heard yourself, and you feel you're ready to give it a try with your child, go to it. Practice leads to confidence and confidence leads to success.

Q&A
FOR PARENTS

Q **What if I try to do Corrective Teaching and my child says he doesn't care what I say and leaves the house?**

A At this point, your child has lost self-control and is unwilling to follow your instructions. In the next chapter, "Teaching Self-Control," we'll discuss how to handle this kind of situation. For now, as long as you feel comfortable your child is safe when he leaves the house, you can wait to continue your teaching and give consequences when he returns.

Q **Sometimes I correct my child for misbehaviors. But when she goes to her father's house for a weekend, she gets away with everything. What am I supposed to do?**

A In a perfect world, both parents would have the same expectations and be consistent with their teaching and use of consequences. But in reality, there is probably very little you can do to change his parenting style. Talk with him about how important it is for you both to have similar expectations for your daughter and to consistently use teaching and consequences for problem behaviors. Also, use Preventive Teaching to help your daughter understand that expectations and rules can change from place to place (school, church, her father's home, etc.). Go over these differences and how she can handle them. You also might encourage her father to read this book or to attend parenting classes.

Q **No consequence I use with Corrective Teaching has any effect on my son's problem behaviors. He just doesn't seem to care.**

A Sometimes it takes a while to find the right consequence — be patient and keep teaching. Also, it's important to remember that consequences alone do not change behaviors; using all of the Common Sense Parenting skills is what will help bring about desired changes in your son's behaviors. So be sure to praise him when he behaves well (Effective Praise) and remind him at neutral times about the behaviors you expect to see him use (Preventive Teaching).

Q **My daughter just ignores everything I say when I correct her. She never stands still for all of these steps.**

A The steps of Corrective Teaching have been designed to help you remain calm and focused on a positive approach to correcting problem behaviors. But it's okay to be flexible when using the steps. In your case, be brief and get to the point. Children, especially younger ones, commonly tune out parents when they get wordy.

Q **If I give my child a negative consequence right away, he just blows up and leaves.**

A Again, be flexible with the steps. You may save the consequence step for the very end so your child has some time to calm down.

Q **My child argues with just about everything I say. She never admits to doing anything wrong, even if I'm specific. She just makes excuses or tries to make me mad when I correct her.**

A Don't allow yourself to get sidetracked during Corrective Teaching. Many children will argue, make excuses, and resort to saying all sorts of things to get your attention away from their problem behaviors and giving them a negative consequence. Stay calm and focus on correcting one problem behavior at a time.

Q **How do I correct my two kids for fighting when I don't know who started it?**

A It takes two to fight, so both children should earn a negative consequence. They may be different consequences, but they should be equal and fair to both. Young children will eventually learn it's wrong to fight, regardless of who starts the fight.

Chapter 11
Teaching Self-Control

One of the more frustrating aspects of parenting is dealing with your child when he or she becomes very angry or defiant or simply refuses to do what you ask. The child may yell, strike out, swear, throw objects, threaten you, or simply shut down and refuse to respond to you at all. Your child's behavior can make you feel powerless, emotionally drained, or just plain furious.

If you have ever felt like this, you're not alone. All parents experience situations like this at one time or another. In fact, some parents face these situations frequently. One thing is certain, however: Kids must learn that negative, aggressive behavior is not acceptable. It is harmful to them and others. The sooner children learn to control their actions, the more they will benefit.

We have developed a teaching method, called **Teaching Self-Control**, that helps parents calmly deal with their children in emotional situations. **Teaching Self-Control enables parents to teach their children better ways to behave when they are upset or refuse to respond to correction. Teaching Self-Control allows everyone time to calm down so teaching can start again.**

185

There are two key parts to Teaching Self-Control: getting your child calmed down and follow-up teaching. We'll talk about each part in detail later. First, let's take a brief look at what often happens when a child yells at a parent or refuses to do what was asked.

In these situations, a child is certainly not interested in, and in some cases, not capable of discussing the situation rationally. A great deal of talking by the parent does little to improve the situation. Often, the more the parent talks, the louder the child yells. The more the child yells, the louder the parent talks — until the parent is yelling, too. This unpleasant exchange of words and actions continues to intensify until someone decides the argument is too painful and drops out. It can be the parent, who walks out of the room in disgust and anger. Or, it can be the child, who stomps off to the bedroom and slams the door shut. In either case, the problem has gotten worse, not better. If you've had to deal with a child who will not cooperate, you know how helpless you can feel during these emotionally intense times.

Teaching Self-Control gives parents a way to stop the yelling or arguing before it gets harmful and before problems get worse. It also provides parents with a structured method for helping kids identify how they're feeling and for teaching them how to deal with these behaviors in ways that are helpful, not hurtful.

When to Use Teaching Self-Control

Teaching Self-Control should be used when children refuse to cooperate with you, either passively or aggressively. Teaching Self-Control is appropriate in these two types of situations:

1. **When a child misbehaves and will not respond to Corrective Teaching; instead, the child continues to misbehave or the misbehavior gets worse.**

2. **When a child "blows up" — has a sudden and intense emotional outburst — and refuses to do anything the parent asks.**

An example of aggressive out-of-control behavior would be a situation where a parent asks his son to get up and get ready for school and the son responds by swearing, shouting at his father to get out of his room, and turning the CD player on full blast. Out-of-control behavior can be passive as well. In the same situation, the son might just simply ignore his dad's repeated requests to get out of bed.

Think about times when your children got upset when you corrected their behavior or asked them to do something. What triggered their negative behavior? What exactly did they do? How did you respond? Looking back at past blow-ups can help you plan for and practice how you will deal with them in the future. Ways to prevent blow-ups include using Preventive Teaching (Chapter 7) to help your child learn more appropriate ways to respond when he or she feels angry or upset, and using your plan for staying calm (Chapter 9). However, once your child does have an emotional outburst, it's time to use the steps of Teaching Self-Control.

The Steps of Teaching Self-Control

Teaching Self-Control has two goals and two parts. The goals of Teaching Self-Control are:

- **To help you and your children calm down during emotionally intense situations.**

- **To teach your children how to control their behavior when they get upset.**

The first part of Teaching Self-Control — Calming Down — is geared toward reducing the intensity of your interaction so both you and your child can work on resolving the situation. The second part — Follow-Up Teaching — gives you an opportunity to teach your child some acceptable options for behaving when he or she is upset. Like the other skills you have learned, Teaching Self-Control emphasizes giving clear descriptions of your child's behaviors, using consequences, teaching your child the desired behavior, providing a reason for using the desired behavior, and practicing it. Teaching Self-Control gives both you and your child a chance to calm down when tempers have flared. When everyone has some time to calm down before teaching continues, kids are more likely to learn how to share their feelings in appropriate and constructive ways. Here are the steps of Teaching Self-Control and an example of how it could be used:

Part One: Calming Down
1. Describe the problem behavior.
2. Offer options to calm down.
3. Allow time to calm down.
4. Check for cooperative behavior.

Part Two: Follow-Up Teaching
5. Describe the desired behavior (Stay Calm).
6. Give a reason.

7. **Practice (Stay Calm).**

8. **Give a negative consequence (for not staying calm).**

Example: Dad and Mom tell their 17-year-old son Jamal he can't use the family computer for the next two weeks because he visited an inappropriate website. Jamal laughs and says, *"I'll just get on it when you're not around! Or I'll go next door and use Steve's computer! You can't stop me!"* He walks away from them, gets on his cell phone, and starts talking to his friend about how stupid his parents are.

Part One: Calming Down

1. **Describe the problem behavior.**

Dad: *"Jamal, I know you want to talk on the phone, but right now you are continuing to talk and laugh instead of following my instructions. Hang up the phone and come to the kitchen."*

        (Jamal continues talking on the phone and doesn't follow his parent's instruction.)

2. **Offer options to calm down.**

Dad: *"Jamal, please follow my instructions and show me you're willing to cooperate by giving me the phone and going to your room to calm down.*

        (Jamal starts to leave the room but continues talking on the phone.)

        "It's up to you to make a better decision about not using the phone. I suggest you take a few deep breaths and

think about what you're doing."

(Jamal stops, ends the phone call, and angrily shoves the phone in front of Dad's face.)

Jamal: *"This is so lame. Just leave me alone!"*

3. Allow time to calm down.

Dad: *"I can see you're still upset.*

(Dad takes the phone.)

Please go to your room and I'll be there in a few minutes to talk."

(When Jamal is following instructions and is willing to talk with his Dad about the problem, Dad moves from the Calming Down phase to the Follow-Up Teaching phase.)

4. Check for cooperative behavior.

Dad: *"Okay, Jamal, you look like you are calmer now. Are you ready to talk this through?"*

Jamal: *"Yeah, I guess."*

Part Two: Follow-Up Teaching

5. Describe the desired behavior (Stay Calm).

Dad: *"Jamal, I know it's sometimes hard to stay calm when you want to do something, but here is what you can do the next time you get upset. I'd like you to use the Staying Calm Plan you agreed on. Take a few deep breaths and calmly*

> *ask me if you can go to your room
> to think. That also means not using
> the phone or playing your music."*

6. Give a reason.

Dad: *"It's important to stay calm because it
will show you are getting more mature."*

7. Practice (Stay Calm).

Dad: *"Let's give this a try. In a little while,
you are going to earn a nega-
tive consequence for losing control
and not following instructions to
stop talking on the phone. Show me
how you are going to handle yourself if you start getting angry."*

Jamal: (Takes a deep breath)

      "Can I go to my room until I feel calm?"

Dad: *"That was exactly what you should do."*

8. Give a negative consequence (for not staying calm).

Dad: *"As I said, you've earned a negative
consequence for losing control and
continuing to use the phone when I
asked you to stop. You won't be allowed to use the phone until you do
three considerate things for me or
your mom for not staying calm."*

It's never easy to remain calm when your child is being openly defiant and disrespectful. What's important is to first focus on helping the child calm down and regain self-control before you address the original problem behavior. (In the example, Dad first handles Jamal's loss of control. Once Jamal is calm, Dad can return to the issue of his son's improper use of the computer.) Each of the steps of Teaching Self-Control is a way for parents to determine if their child is ready to cooperate and eventually get back to the initial problem that caused the blow-up in the first place. These steps not only act as markers of your child's ability to remain calm, but also give parents a proven method to avoid being drawn into power struggles, arguments that can escalate, or what could become an unsafe family situation.

Now, let's look at the steps of the first part of Teaching Self-Control — Calming Down — in more detail.

STEP 1: Describe the Problem Behavior

Using empathy helps when your child is upset or angry. It shows you understand your child's feelings. For example, you might say, *"I can see you are angry right now. And your voice tells me you're unhappy with what happened."* This starts the teaching sequence positively and shows your child you really do care about his or her feelings. Plus, using empathy often helps your child see you're focused on calming the situation down and not on placing blame or getting the upper hand.

In a calm, level voice tone, *briefly* tell your child exactly what he or she is doing wrong. Your child probably will not be interested in listening to what you have to say at this time, so saying a lot won't help. Remember that you will have time to describe the problem in detail once your child settles down. For now, be clear and specific with what you say. Don't speak too rapidly or say too much; for example, saying, *"Marcus, I know you are upset, but you are pacing around the room,"* gives the child a clear message about what he is doing.

Parents often say judgmental things when they dislike their child's behavior, such as *"Quit acting like a brat"* or *"I hate your lousy attitude."* However, these critical, judgmental statements only serve to fuel the emotional fire in your child. We suggest that you simply describe what your child is doing wrong without becoming angry, sarcastic, or accusatory.

STEP 2: Offer Options to Calm Down

The purpose of this step is to tell your child exactly what he or she needs to do to begin calming down. Give simple instructions like, *"Please go to your room until you are calm"* or *"Go sit on the porch and cool down."* Or, make calming statements to prompt your child: *"Take a few deep breaths and try to settle down."* Just as when you described the problem behavior, keep your words to a minimum. Don't give too many instructions or repeat them constantly; your child could perceive this as lecturing, badgering, or an opportunity to argue. Giving simple, clear options for calming down keeps the focus on having your child regain self-control.

It is very important that you practice these first two steps. Practicing how to be brief, specific, calm, empathetic, and clear during intense situations is time well invested. Besides giving your child an opportunity to regain self-control, giving clear messages and specific options on how to calm down helps you avoid getting sidetracked into useless arguments or power struggles.

STEP 3: Allow Time to Calm Down

It's probably safe to say giving children time to calm down may be a new concept to many parents. But if you remain calm and allow your children time to cool down, they are more likely to get themselves together faster. Parents tell us that remembering this step has helped them stay focused on getting the situation under control. Simply saying, *"Let's take a little time to calm down. I'll be back in a few minutes,"* can be surprisingly effective. Sometimes, giving you and your child a little "space" helps you both "save face."

As you take time to calm down, you can think of what you are going to teach next. This also allows your child to make a decision — to continue misbehaving or to calm down. Come back to the child as often as necessary to ask questions like, *"Are you ready to talk about what happened?"* or *"Are you calmed down enough to talk to me?"*

Move to the next phase, Follow-up Teaching, when your child is able to answer you in a reasonably calm voice and is willing to cooperate. You're not going to have the happiest child at this point, but it's important that he or she can pay attention and talk to you without losing self-control again.

If your child tries to use this "cool down time" as an opportunity to blare music, sleep, talk on the phone, or go from room to room disrupting others, then you should remind your child those behaviors will only make things worse for him or her later. For example, if your daughter gets upset when you tell her to turn off the TV and then refuses to stop watching, part of her consequence will be losing TV time. Don't make angry threats; simply inform your child that continued misbehavior will earn larger or more negative consequences. This is a good time to prompt your child to make better decisions and to give a brief reason that's meaningful to him or her.

STEP 4: Check for Cooperative Behavior

It's important to take your time here. Give descriptions and instructions as needed to test your child's readiness to move on to Follow-Up Teaching. Most importantly, remain calm and in control of what you say and do.

Here is a more detailed look at the steps of Follow-Up Teaching.

STEP 5: Describe the Desired Behavior (Stay Calm)

Describe what your child can do differently next time to remain calm. Explain other, more positive ways to express frustration or anger. Children have to learn that if they blow up when something doesn't go their way, it leads to more negative consequences and less time for doing the things they like. This is an opportunity to explain the prompts you gave in the "Offer Options to Cool Down" step and to encourage your child to remember how to calm down.

We teach many parents to use the **"Instead of..."** phrase to describe positive behavior. It goes like this:

- *"Instead of yelling and running out the door, the next time you get upset, please tell me you're mad and ask if you can go to your room to calm down."*

- *"Instead of swearing, why don't you ask if you can sit on the porch until you are ready to talk about it."*

The purpose of this phrase is to teach children these are positive behaviors they can use the next time they get upset.

Part of this teaching can include helping them recognize when they are beginning to get upset and teaching them to say something like, *"I'm getting mad. Can I have some time to calm down?"*

Once children calm down, they can talk about the circumstances that triggered their anger and talk with you about a solution. If parents and kids can learn to talk about how they feel in these situations, they can successfully solve the problem rather than attack each other.

STEP 6: Give a Reason

Giving a reason will help teach your child why it's important to stay calm in a difficult situation; for example, *"Staying calm makes it easier for us to discuss your concerns."* Reasons are most effective when they are personal to the child, related to the staying calm skill, and can be used in different situations. It's also helpful to avoid promising outcomes by using "possibility" words such as *"...it's more likely."*

STEP 7: Practice (Stay Calm)

Now that your child knows what to do, it's important that he or she knows how to do it. Ask your child to take several deep breaths with you, count to 10, or repeat a request for time to calm down, such as *"I'm really upset right now. May I go to my room for a few minutes?"* After the practice is over, let your child know what he or she did correctly and what needs improvement. Be as positive as you can be, especially if your child is making an honest effort to do what you ask. Practice allows you to see if your child is in control of his or her emotions and is willing to cooperate with your instructions as well as accept responsibility for the behavior.

STEP 8: Give a Negative Consequence (for not staying calm)

This is a crucial step to Teaching Self-Control. If there is a common mistake made by parents we work with, it is that they forget to give a negative consequence for the out-of-control behavior. Some tell us they are so pleased to have the yelling stop that giving a consequence doesn't cross their minds. Other parents say they don't give a negative consequence because they don't want to upset their child any further. Sometimes, after a blow-up is over, parents want to ease up on their child or the child's remorse convinces the parents to skip giving the consequence. These feelings are understandable, but they don't contribute to changing a child's behavior. Consequences do help change behavior, but only if they are consistently used.

With Teaching Self-Control, you should always give an appropriate negative consequence and follow through with it. Children must learn they cannot blow up or throw tantrums when things don't go their way. At school, these behaviors can result in detentions, suspensions, expulsions, or other disciplinary actions. At work, they could cost a teen his or her job. And most likely, children won't keep friends for very long if they can't control their tempers. As parents, we must teach children how to respond in less emotional and less harmful ways even when they get upset. Consequences increase the effectiveness of your teaching, and the whole process of Teaching Self-Control helps your children learn better ways of behaving.

Example of Teaching Self-Control

Let's take a look at another example of Teaching Self-Control. Here's the situation: Mom tells her 10-year-old son

Alex he can't go over to a friend's house because he didn't come straight home after school as she requested. He yells, "That's so stupid! I hate you! You never let me do anything!" Then, he stomps into the family room, screaming and swearing.

Part One: Calming Down

1. **Describe the problem behavior.**

   - Start with praise or empathy.
   - Describe the out-of-control behavior.

   > Mom: *"I can see it's hard for you to accept not being able to go to your friend's house, but you are yelling and swearing."*

2. **Offer options to calm down.**

   - Give choices.
   - Specifically describe how to calm down.

   > Mom: *"Please stop yelling and either go to your room or stay out here and sit on the couch. Whatever you decide, take a deep breath and try to calm down."*

3. **Allow time to calm down.**

   - Allow space.
   - Allow time.
   - Monitor.

4. **Check for cooperative behavior.**

   > Mom: *"Alex, how are you feeling now? Are you ready to calmly talk to me?"*

or *"I can see that you're still upset. I'll be back in a few minutes."*

(When Alex is following Mom's instructions and is willing to talk about the problem, Mom can move from the Calming Down phase to the Follow-Up Teaching phase.)

Part Two: Follow-Up Teaching

5. Describe the desired behavior (Stay Calm).

- Think of a better way your child can react when he gets upset. Describe what he can do differently.

Mom: *"Here's what you can do the next time you get upset, Alex. What I'd like you to do is let me know that you are getting upset and ask me if you can go to your room and calm down."*

6. Give a reason.

Mom: *"If you can stay calm, it will help us work through this quicker."*

7. Practice (Stay Calm).

- Clearly set up practice.
- Have the child practice to criteria.
- Provide feedback.

Mom: *"Okay, let's practice this. I'm going to tell you you can't go out and play. What should you do?"*

Alex: *"Mom, I feel really mad right now. Can I go to my room until I feel calm?"*

Mom: *"That was great, Alex! You asked me in a nice tone of voice."*

8. Give a negative consequence (for not staying calm).

- Help prevent the problem from occurring again.

Mom: *"Remember, there are negative consequences for yelling and swearing. Tonight, you'll have to do the dinner dishes and you won't get a snack."*

In real-life situations, your child probably won't cooperate this quickly. He or she may go from arguing and swearing to being calm, and then suddenly start arguing again. Some kids have a lot of stamina when they're upset so it's best to realize it could take a while to resolve the problem. You may also have other distractions to deal with in these situations: Your other children need something, the phone rings, the soup is boiling over on the stove, and so on. Interactions with your child do not occur in a void; other things are always taking place that affect your behavior. In those instances where other children are present, use the Safe Home Plan you learned about in Chapter 9, "Staying Calm," and adapt the teaching steps and your teaching style to the situation. Stick to simple descriptions and instructions, continue to use empathy, and stay calm. Also, when children misuse privileges when they're upset (blaring music on their Smartphone), they should lose access to those privileges (no Smartphone the rest of the day) as part of the consequence.

Helpful Hints

Stay on task.

Don't lose sight of what you're trying to teach. Implement all of the steps of Teaching Self-Control. Concentrating on your child's behavior is much easier when you have a framework to follow. Teaching Self-Control gives you that framework. It helps you stay calm and avoid arguments that take you away from what you want to teach.

Your children may try to argue with what you say or call you names. They may say you don't love them or tell you how unfair you are. They may say things to make you feel guilty or angry or useless. Expect these statements but don't respond to them. If you get caught up in all of these side issues, you lose sight of your original purpose — to calm your child and teach him or her self-control. And, you can lose sight of the original problem and how you need to deal with it. If you find yourself responding to what your child is saying, remember to use a key phrase: *"We'll talk about that when you calm down."* Staying on task ensures you won't start arguing or losing your temper.

Be aware of your physical actions.

These times can be emotionally explosive. Don't use threatening words or gestures that might encourage physical retaliation from your child. Some parents find that sitting down rather than standing helps to calm the situation. When parents stand up — particularly fathers — children see them as more threatening. Any action your child views as aggressive will only make matters worse and reduce the likelihood he or she will calm down.

Pointing your index finger, putting your hands on your hips, scowling, leaning over your child, and raising a fist are all examples of physical actions that tend to increase tension in these volatile situations. Try your best to avoid these gestures. Keep your hands in your pockets or fold your arms across your chest — just find something to do with your hands and arms other than waving them at your child.

Plan consequences in advance.

Think of a variety of appropriate negative consequences beforehand, especially if losing self-control is a problem for your child. Making decisions when you are upset can lead to giving huge consequences you can't follow through with.

Find time when your child is not upset to explain the consequence for arguing and fighting with you. For example, you might say, *"Sarah, when I tell you 'No,' sometimes you argue with me. Then you get real mad and start yelling. From now on, if you do this, you will lose your phone and texting privileges for two nights."* Then explain to Sarah why she needs to accept decisions and why she shouldn't argue or scream. Knowing what the consequence will be may help your child think and try to stay calm rather than losing self-control in the future.

Follow up.

As your child calms down and you complete the teaching sequence, other side issues can arise. Some situations may call for an understanding approach. Kids may cry after an intense situation. They just don't know how to handle what they're feeling inside. Then you can say, *"Let's sit down and talk about why you've been feeling so angry. Maybe I can help. At least, I can listen."*

Some children enjoy "making up" with parents after an emotionally intense situation. In these situations, use a firm, emphatic ending to Teaching Self-Control and keep your follow-up brief. This discourages them from losing control again and allows them to engage in hugs and kisses once everything calms down. Simply indicate that the child's behavior was unacceptable and the interaction is finished: *"Okay, you've practiced what you should do next time. Now, go to your brother's room and apologize to him."*

Whatever approach you take will be determined by your common sense and judgment. It depends entirely on how you feel about the situation and what you want to teach.

Earlier, we emphasized you shouldn't get sidetracked by the complaints and accusations kids may bring up when they are angry. But that's only during the Teaching Self-Control process. Afterwards, when everyone has calmed down, you should discuss with your child those statements that upset or concerned you. This is your opportunity to find out the reasons behind the outburst.

Kids may make more negative comments during these emotionally intense situations, especially when you first start using Teaching Self-Control, because these comments may have distracted you before. They may think they can avoid getting a consequence or doing what was asked if they just keep the pressure on you. In other situations, kids may make these comments because they sincerely don't know how to express their feelings in healthy ways. Sometimes, children later tell their parents they made negative comments just because they were mad. Other times, kids really do have concerns, or they feel frustrated. Some children won't have a clue why they said what they did, but discussing it and allowing them to share their feelings helps the healing begin.

When you have finished Teaching Self-Control and both you and your child are calm, you may want to discuss some of these comments. Tell your child you're concerned about what he or she said. Talk about trust. Ask your child to share his or her feelings and opinions with you. Regardless of why the comments were made, take time to hear what your child has to say. Whenever possible, implement the suggestions the child makes. By doing so, you will be opening the door to more constructive conversations with your child. You will also be reducing the likelihood your child will express negative feelings in destructive ways.

Also, parents need to share how they feel with their children and let them know that they need to be able to trust them. This open dialogue provides parents and children with a safe and more effective way to communicate what they really think without feeling hurt or rejected. Working through these rough times together forms the tightest emotional bonds between you and your kids.

Finally, as part of following up, you should sit down with your child at a neutral time (when he or she is not upset) and develop a Staying Calm Plan for the child. Help your child go through the same steps you followed in developing a plan for yourself (Chapter 9): Identify what upsets him or her and select a method for calming down. Having a plan of their own helps children recognize when they are beginning to feel upset and gives them specific methods for staying calm. Then, when you must use Teaching Self-Control, your child may need only a prompt from you to realize it's time to get his or her negative emotions under control.

Summary

Parents must have a bountiful supply of patience if their children have a problem with self-control. The wisest parents are those who realize teaching their kids self-control is an ongoing process. It takes a long time. Don't try to rush the learning process; expecting too much too soon can create more problems than it solves. Be attentive to small accomplishments; praise even the smallest bit of progress your child makes. (And, while you're at it, give yourself a big pat on the back. Using Teaching Self-Control is a tough job.)

Look for small positive changes over time. Your child should have fewer angry outbursts, and the outbursts should be shorter and not nearly as intense. Teaching Self-Control helps parents and children break the painful cycle of arguments and power struggles. When tension is greatest in the family, Teaching Self-Control gives everyone a constructive way to resolve problems.

☞ CHAPTER REVIEW

What are the two parts of Teaching Self-Control?

Calming Down and Follow-Up Teaching

When should parents use Teaching Self-Control?

1. When children misbehave and do not respond to Corrective Teaching.

2. When children blow up and refuse to do what a parent asks.

What happens if a child uses privileges when he or she loses self-control?

The child should lose access to those privileges later as part of the consequence.

☆ ACTION PLAN

1. Take some time to answer the following questions:

   • What is the most important thing you learned in this chapter?

   • What do you plan to do differently as a result of what you've learned?

2. Think about situations where your child has lost control in the past. Choose the situation that you think is most likely to occur again. On a sheet of paper, list the steps to Teaching Self-Control and then write out a scenario for what you can say or do for each step to handle the situation. Look back at the scenario and consider what you will do if your child refuses to calm down easily. What will you suggest that your child do to calm down? What consequence do you think will be most effective? What will you do to stay calm?

   Practice the steps with your spouse or a friend so you feel more comfortable saying the words with your child. Refer to your scenario several times in the days to come so that if your child does lose control, you will be prepared to handle the situation.

Q&A
FOR PARENTS

Q **Is the consequence I give in Teaching Self-Control for not following instructions, like my son not making his bed, or for the tantrum that follows?**

A Your son should earn a consequence for his tantrum. Later, when he is calm, you can again teach your son how to follow instructions. If you had originally given him a consequence for not following instructions, that consequence should stand as well as the consequence for losing control.

Q **What if I send my child to her room to calm down and she stays there all night?**

A If she decides to stay in her room all night, that's okay. Just check on her regularly to make sure she's safe. If she hasn't calmed down or is unable to work things out before bedtime, let her go to sleep and finish Follow-Up Teaching the next morning. You shouldn't keep a child up all night, especially a young one. Sometimes, a good night's sleep is the best medicine to help a child calm down. But it's important to do the Follow-Up Teaching.

Q **What should my daughter do when I give her some time to go get herself together?**

A She should do something that helps her calm down. Some suggestions are: listening to soothing music, taking deep breaths, counting to 100, writing in a journal, or going for a walk. Remember to use Preventive Teaching to work out a Staying Calm Plan with your daughter before intense situations occur so you both know what to do.

207

Q What if my child blows up in the morning when I have to go to work and he has to go to school?

A You have two choices: Either send him to school and pick up your teaching later (after work) where you left off, or call the school and your workplace to let them know you and your son will be late, and take care of the situation right away. It will depend on how upset your child is and if you think he can go to school without causing more problems.

Q What if my child gets angry and strikes me or someone else?

A After you feel confident that you, your child, and others are safe, take a break and get away from your child for a bit. You need time to collect yourself. Never corner or aggressively approach your child, especially when he or she has a tendency to lash out when upset or angry. Always work on trying to stay calm. Remember, your child will earn a consequence for the misbehaviors after he or she is calm and you do Follow-Up Teaching.

Q How do I know when my daughter has calmed down enough to move to Follow-Up Teaching?

A She should be able to follow some simple instructions, such as "Let's go to the kitchen to talk" or "Please sit down here." If she follows your instructions, you can move to Follow-Up Teaching. If she doesn't follow your instructions, she's not calm enough and you'll need to give her more time to calm down.

SECTION IV
PUTTING IT ALL TOGETHER

So far, we've presented a number of valuable parenting skills that focus on how and what to teach children, the importance of building strong relationships with your children, and how to develop a parenting style that is both firm and caring. We hope you have been practicing and using these skills with your children.

In this section, we will promote two concepts that are crucial to better parenting: making your new parenting skills part of your daily family life and your parenting "personality," and agreeing on and committing to the parenting approach (or style) you are going to use from now on.

This can be accomplished through teaching your children social skills; developing activities such as Family Meetings, routines, and traditions; making decisions together; and creating a plan for better parenting. We will provide advice and suggestions for these things, but how you implement them in your family will ultimately reflect who you are as a parent and the changes you choose to make in your approach to parenting.

Change requires patience. It isn't always easy, and it can mean many adjustments in a family. Obviously, the age of your children will determine how you use your new skills, and that will change as your kids get older. Also, as you change your parenting style, the role you play in your children's lives will take on a different dimension; there will be more interactions, you will know when to hold back and when to step in, and your parenting will become more fluid.

The main goal in all this is to fashion and adopt a parenting approach that incorporates all of the teaching skills you've learned and to totally commit to that approach. Once you learn new ways of parenting, it is important to make them part of who you are and your family's value system. This commitment is the first step in deciding you are going to break the cycle of how you used to parent and change the things that weren't working well. And while teaching children new ways to behave through effective parenting will have an immediate impact on relationships and behavior within your family, it also models an effective and caring parenting style your children can turn to when they have children of their own. In this way, Common Sense Parenting creates a solid foundation for future generations of parents.

Earlier in the book, we discussed disciplining children through teaching. The activities and concepts in this section will enable you to move from simply disciplining your children to helping them learn how to discipline themselves. This is where all of the tools and skills come together to make parents and children partners in the process of positive self-discipline. Self-discipline involves making good decisions, taking responsibility for one's actions, and knowing when and how to use different social skills in different situations. Children who can do this are better prepared for the future, both while they are living at home and when they get out on their own.

Chapter 12
Teaching Social Skills

⟶

T he Common Sense Parenting skills we have covered so far focus on the "how" of effectively teaching kids; social skills are "what" you should teach.

Social skills are sets of specific behaviors linked together in a certain order. When social skills are used correctly and at the right time, they help us get along with other people and make appropriate decisions in social situations. Think a minute about what you do when you meet someone for the first time. You probably stand up straight, look at the person, smile, give a firm handshake, and say your name and something like "It's nice to meet you." That's an example of how specific behaviors are strung together to make up the social skill of "Introducing Yourself."

We use social skills every day — greeting co-workers, asking a clerk for help, telephoning a friend, talking to a salesperson about a product, giving someone a compliment. The list goes on and on. Using these skills appropriately greatly influences how other people treat us and how we get along in the world. If we have learned a wide variety of social skills, we can effectively handle more situations and get along better with more people.

Obviously, it is essential for children to learn social skills, too. Social skills define for them what behavior is acceptable or unacceptable when interacting with other people and society in general. For parents, social skills provide a framework for teaching children how to behave.

You can teach your children social skills by using Preventive Teaching and Corrective Teaching. When your kids use skills appropriately or make an attempt to use them, you can reward and reinforce their efforts through Effective Praise. In other words, you pick the teaching technique that best fits the situation you're in with your kids. In fact, the steps of each social skill usually neatly fit into the steps of whatever Common Sense Parenting teaching method you are using. This enables you to teach children how, why, and where they should use these skills.

When your kids can use social skills appropriately, they are more likely to know what to do or say when they deal with other people and be more successful in their interactions. Parents who actively teach social skills to their children are equipping them with "survival skills" for getting along with others, for learning self-control, and generally, for having a successful life.

What Should I Teach?

Let's look at some examples of how parents can use Common Sense Parenting techniques to teach or praise the use of social skills.

- Mom asks Jeremy to take out the trash and he responds with, *"Why do I always have to do it?"* Mom can use Corrective Teaching to teach the social skill of "Following Instructions."

- Michelle and her dad are sitting at the dinner table when she begins telling him about a friend who was drinking beer at last night's football game. Dad can use Effective Praise to reinforce the social skill of "Being Honest."

- Dad is in the kitchen when Troy rushes in and says he's going to a friend's house. Dad says dinner is almost ready, so he needs to stay home. Troy begins complaining. Dad can use Corrective Teaching to teach the social skill of "Accepting 'No' for an Answer."

- Nicole has had a problem understanding her math homework in the past. Before she begins her homework, her mom reminds her how to ask for help with problems she doesn't understand. Mom has used Preventive Teaching to encourage Nicole to use the social skill of "Asking for Help."

In each of these examples, the parents taught a specific social skill that will help their children in future situations.

Later in this chapter, we will present a more detailed explanation of 16 important social skills. The helpful hints and reasons that accompany these social skills provide examples of what you can say to your children as you teach these skills. The behaviors listed for each of the skills are general guidelines; they can be changed to fit what you feel your children need to learn.

Children will use social skills many times each day to help them do well at home and in school. More importantly, mastering these skills will be the key to their ability to achieve success and avoid conflicts with others.

Since children learn at different rates, you may need to alter your teaching from child to child, even if they're close to the same age. Some children catch on right away; others require more practice and repetition in order to really learn what you're teaching. Some children don't have the attention span for a lengthy teaching session. Feel free to adjust and modify the steps of the social skills based on your child's ability.

Using Preventive Teaching to Teach Social Skills

Let's look at an example of a mother using Preventive Teaching to teach her 10-year-old how to accept a "No" answer. In the past, when her son was told "No," he would frequently argue, whine, or pout. These behaviors have caused problems not only at home but also in school.

The steps of the skill of "Accepting 'No' for an Answer" are:

1. **Look at the person.**
2. **Say "Okay."**
3. **Calmly ask for a reason if you really don't understand.**
4. **If you disagree, bring it up later.**

Here's how Preventive Teaching might sound in this situation.

1. Describe the desired behavior.

Mom: *"Jimmy, I want to talk with you about how to accept 'No' answers, especially from your teacher. The first thing you need to do is look at her. Don't look away or look down. Okay?"*

Jimmy: *"Uh huh."*

Mom: *"After you look at her, you need to say 'Okay' in a nice voice. If you really don't understand why you were told 'No,' calmly ask for a reason, but only if you don't understand. If you disagree with the answer, politely bring it up later."*

2. Give a reason.

Mom: *"If you learn how to accept a 'No' answer without arguing, your teacher is more likely to listen to what you have to say. Do you understand?"*

Jimmy: *"Yeah, Mom. Are we done?"*

3. Practice.

Mom: *"Not quite. Let's pretend I'm Mrs. Smith and you're going to ask me to use the computer...."*

Mom and Jimmy would practice this situation or others he might face during school. As Jimmy practices, Mom can see where he does well and where he struggles. For example, maybe his voice tone sounds rather harsh or negative or he fidgets when he talks. Mom can practice with Jimmy until he feels more comfortable with each step of the skill. She also can provide real-life reasons for why learning this social skill will make things go smoother for him.

Notice that Mom picked a time to use Preventive Teaching when Jimmy was cooperative and wasn't busy doing something else. She used a calm, conversational tone and continued to ask Jimmy if he understood what she was teaching.

Using Corrective Teaching to Teach Social Skills

In situations where you are correcting your child's inappropriate behavior, Corrective Teaching works best to teach social skills. For example, let's say Dad heard 9-year-old Rita call her sister names like "stupid" and "idiot." Here's an example of how Corrective Teaching could be used to teach the skill of "Asking for Help."

1. **Stop/Describe the problem behavior.**

    Dad: *"Rita, when I walked into the room, I heard you call Tammy names like 'stupid' and 'idiot.' I'm sure that hurt her feelings, don't you think?"*

    Rita: *"But Dad, she was bugging me."*

    Dad: *"That may be true, but calling her names isn't the way to take care of it."*

2. **Give a negative consequence.**

    Dad: *"For calling Tammy names, I want you to apologize to her and then help her clean up the toys in her bedroom."*

    Rita: *"Oh, all right."*

3. **Describe the desired behavior.**

    Dad: *"When Tammy is bugging you, decide exactly what it is that bothers you. Then ask her to stop. If she continues to do things that bother you, come to Mom or me and ask for help in solving the problem. Okay?"*

    Rita: *"Okay."*

Dad: *"When you need to ask someone for help, you should look at the person, say exactly what the problem is, ask for help in a calm voice, and thank the person for helping afterwards. Does that make sense?"*

Rita: *"Yeah, I guess so."*

4. Give a reason.

Dad: *"If you tell Tammy what is bugging you, and ask her politely to stop, she is more likely to listen to you. Do you understand?"*

Rita: *"Yes."*

5. Practice.

Dad: *"Before you apologize, show me how you would ask me for help if Tammy is bothering you."*

Rita: *"Okay. I would look at you and say something to you like 'Daddy, Tammy keeps grabbing my toys and sticking her tongue out at me. I asked her to stop but she wouldn't. Can you help me?' After you helped me, I would tell you 'Thanks.'"*

Dad: *"Great job! Now go tell your sister you're sorry."*

Always make the steps of the skill easy to understand and make sure they fit your child's age, developmental level, and abilities. If your children are younger or have a hard time remembering each step, you can teach and practice the first two steps until your kids understand them completely, then add the other two later.

Teaching your kids social skills can help them build strong relationships with others and with you. When teaching these skills, use simple explanations and examples your child will understand. Use Effective Praise when you see your child attempting to use a skill, showing improvement, or using a skill appropriately.

Helpful Hints

Teach each of the skills step by step.

Try to include a brief pause following each step that gives your child time to process the information. Take time to explain to your children when they can use these skills and give positive child-oriented reasons for how and why these skills will help them. Let them see how one skill overlaps into other areas. For example, knowing how to accept criticism from parents is very similar to accepting criticism from other adult authority figures such as a teacher or coach.

Make learning social skills fun.

Praise your children or reward them with something special for taking the time to learn. They might not realize the benefits of learning social skills right away. But the more they use these skills and see the positive way other people respond to them, the more the skills will "sink in."

Finally, be patient.

After your children learn a new skill, it may take a while before they are comfortable using it and before it really becomes a part of them. Learning new skills is an ongoing process. It's not a "done deal" just because skills have been practiced once or twice. Comparisons can be drawn to almost any other skill we learn. You don't learn how to dribble a basketball in one try; you don't learn how to drive a car the first time you climb behind the wheel. We don't become good at anything without practice, practice, practice.

Summary

Social skills give your children a solid foundation for getting along with others and being more successful in many areas of their lives. Kids of all ages can benefit. Young children, grade-schoolers, and teenagers all can learn skills like "Following Instructions" and "Giving Compliments." Don't hesitate to teach your children acceptable ways to behave. The time to begin teaching social skills is now.

This chapter includes 16 basic social skills all children should learn and master. Remember that when you teach these skills, you must use wording and explanations that fit your child's age, developmental level, and abilities.

☞ CHAPTER REVIEW

What are social skills?

Social skills are sets of specific behaviors linked together in a certain order.

Why do children need to learn social skills?

Social skills define for kids what behavior is acceptable or unacceptable when interacting with other people and society in general. Social skills provide a framework for teaching children how to behave.

☆ ACTION PLAN

1. Take some time to answer the following questions:
   - What is the most important thing you learned in this chapter?
   - What do you plan to do differently as a result of what you learned?

2. Make an effort to use the things you learned from this chapter in your family's everyday life. Have a Social Skill Spree week. After a group discussion, decide on a "target social skill" for each family member. The goal of the week is for each family member to try to use their target social skill as many times as possible with other family members.

   Each day, parents and children can share at family meal time how they've used the social skill that day. Use a chart to keep track of progress. On the seventh day, the child who has recorded the most frequent use of his or her target social skill can choose a fun activity from a list you have created and approved.

Q&A

FOR PARENTS

Q How can I get my son to use the skills I teach him with his friends?

A You can't force him to generalize the social skills he practices at home, but you can encourage his efforts to use his skills with friends. Try making his contact with friends contingent on his ability to use his social skills in other places. For example, if your son comes home on time from an outing with his friends, praise him for following instructions.

Q My daughter doesn't pay attention long enough for me to teach her a social skill. What can I do?

A If your child has a short attention span or often daydreams, then make your steps brief and your teaching concise. Keep her engaged by asking her if she understands what you've said, having her repeat the steps and tell you how the skill will help her.

Q What if my child doesn't use a social skill even after we've talked about it and practiced it?

A Getting children to buy into using skills is never easy and will not happen overnight. Some children don't fully understand the use of social skills; others don't see how social skills will help them. A few children won't want to use social skills because they are being openly defiant. In any case, parents should be patient and use all their parenting skills to encourage their children's cooperation. Try using positive consequences early on to reward your child when he or she does use a skill appropriately.

Following Instructions

When you are given an instruction, you should:

1. **Look at the person who is talking.**
2. **Show you understand.**
   (Say, *"I understand,"* *"Okay,"* or *"I'll do it."*)
   Make sure you wait until the person is done talking before you do what is asked. It is usually best to answer, but sometimes nodding your head will be enough to show the person you understand.
3. **Do what is asked in the best way you can.**
4. **Check back** with the person to let him or her know you have finished.

Reasons for using the skill: It is important that you do what is asked because it shows you can cooperate and lets you get back to doing the things you like to do. Following instructions will help you in school, at home, and with adults and friends.

Helpful Hints

- After you know exactly what you've been asked to do, start the task immediately.
- If you think doing what is asked will result in some type of negative consequence for you, or you don't understand, ask a trusted adult.
- Do what is asked as pleasantly as possible.
- Check back as soon as you finish. This increases the chances you will get credit for doing a job well. It also means somebody else won't have time to mess up what you did before you check back.

ACCEPTING CRITICISM

When others tell you how they think you can improve, they give you criticism. To accept criticism appropriately:

1. **Look at the person.**
   Don't use negative facial expressions.
2. **Stay calm and quiet while the person is talking.**
3. **Show you understand.**
   (Say, *"Okay"* or *"I understand."*)
4. **Try to correct the problem.**
   If you are asked to do something differently, do it. If you are asked to stop doing something, stop it. If you can't give a positive response, at least give one that will not get you into trouble. (Say, *"Okay,"* *"I understand,"* or *"Thanks."*)

Reasons for using the skill: Being able to accept criticism shows you can accept responsibility for what you do and accept advice from others. It also prevents having problems with people in authority. If you can control yourself and listen to what others have to say about how you can improve, you'll have fewer problems. And, the criticism may really help you!

Helpful Hints

- It is most important you stay calm. Take a deep breath, if necessary.

- Getting angry or making negative facial expressions will only get you into trouble.

- When you respond to the person who is giving you criticism, use as pleasant a voice tone as possible. You will receive criticism for the rest of your life — all people do. The way you handle it determines how you are treated by others.

- Most criticism is designed to help you; however, it is sometimes hard to accept. If you don't agree with the criticism, ask Mom, Dad, or another trusted adult.

- Always ask questions if you don't understand. (But don't play games by asking questions when you do understand and are just being stubborn.) Give yourself a chance to improve!

ACCEPTING 'NO' FOR AN ANSWER

1. **Look at the person.**
2. **Say "Okay."**
3. **Calmly ask for a reason** if you really don't understand.
4. **If you disagree, bring it up later.**

Reasons for using the skill: You will be told *"No"* many times in your life. Getting angry and upset only leads to more problems. If you are able to appropriately accept a "No" answer, people might be more likely to say *"Yes"* to your requests in the future.

Helpful Hints

- Don't stare, make faces, or look away. If you are upset, control your emotions. Try to relax and stay calm. Listening carefully will help you understand what the other person is saying.

- Answer right away and speak clearly. Take a deep breath if you feel upset.

- Don't ask for a reason every time or you will be viewed as a complainer. People will think you are serious about wanting to know a reason if you ask for one calmly. Don't keep asking for reasons after you receive one. Use what you learn in these situations in the future.

- Take some time to plan how you are going to approach the person who told you *"No."* Plan in advance what you are going to say. Accept the answer, even if it is still *"No."* Be sure to thank the person for listening. At least you had the opportunity to share your opinion.

STAYING CALM

When people feel angry or upset, it's hard to stay calm. When we feel like "blowing up," we sometimes make poor choices. And usually when we make poor choices, we regret it later. If you feel you are going to lose self-control, you should:

1. **Take a deep breath.**
2. **Relax** your muscles.
3. Tell yourself to **"Be calm," or count to ten.**
4. **Share your feelings.** After you are relaxed, tell someone you trust what is bothering you.
5. **Try to solve the situation** that made you upset.

Reasons for using the skill: It is important to stay calm since worse things always seem to happen if you lose your temper. If you can stay calm, other people will depend on you more often. They will see you as someone who is able to handle bad situations. Teachers and employers will respect you and see you as someone who can keep his or her "cool."

Helpful Hints

- Don't try to talk yourself into the idea that "blowing up" is the only thing to do, or that the person or thing that is upsetting you "deserves it." Forget it. It doesn't work that way. And, you're setting yourself up to get more or worse consequences. Be calm.

- After you have calmed down, pat yourself on the back. Even adults have a hard time with self-control. If you can control yourself, you will have accomplished something many adults are still struggling with. Give yourself some praise! You have done the right thing.

⋏ DISAGREEING WITH OTHERS

When you don't agree with another person's opinion or decision, you should:

1. **Remain calm.**
   Getting upset will only make matters worse.
2. **Look at the person.**
   This shows you have confidence.

3. **Begin with a positive or neutral statement.**
   "I know you are trying to be fair, but...."
4. **Explain why you disagree** with the opinion or decision. Keep your voice tone level and controlled. Be brief and clear.
5. **Listen as the other person** explains his or her side of the story.
6. **If the other person's opinion or decision cannot be changed, calmly accept it.**
7. **Thank the person for listening,** regardless of the outcome.

Reasons for using the skill: It is important to disagree in a calm manner because it increases the chances the other person will listen to you. This may be the only opportunity you have to challenge an opinion or get a decision changed. You have a right to express your opinions. But you lose that right if you become upset or aggressive. If the other person feels you are going to lose self-control, you stand very little chance of getting your views across.

Helpful Hints

- You're not going to win every time. Some opinions or decisions will not change. However, learning how to disagree calmly may help change some of them.

- Don't try to change everything. People will view you as a pest.

- If you are calm and specific when you disagree, people will respect you for the mature way you handle situations. It pays off in the long run!

ASKING FOR HELP

When you need help with something, you should:

1. **Decide what the problem is.**
2. **Ask to speak to the person** who is most likely to help you.
3. **Look at the person, clearly describe what you need help with, and ask the person in a pleasant voice tone.**
4. **Thank the person** for helping you.

Reasons for using the skill: It is important to ask others for help because it is the best way to solve problems you can't figure out. Asking for help in a pleasant manner makes it more likely someone will help you.

Helpful Hints

- Although it is nice to figure things out by yourself, sometimes this isn't possible. Asking someone who has more experience, or has had more success with a similar problem, is a way to learn how to solve the problem the next time.

- Sometimes, people become frustrated, and even get mad, when they can't figure something out. Learn to ask for help before you get to this point and you will have more successes than failures.

- Always tell the person who is helping you how much you appreciate the help. It might be nice to offer your help the next time that person needs something.

ASKING PERMISSION

When you need to get permission from someone, you should:

1. **Look at the other person.**
2. **Be specific** when you ask permission.
   The other person should know exactly what you are requesting.
3. Be sure to **ask rather than demand.**
   "May I please...?"
4. **Give reasons** if necessary.
5. **Accept the decision.**

Reasons to use the skill: It is important to ask permission whenever you want to do something or use something another person is responsible for. Asking permission shows your respect for others and increases the chances your request will be granted.

Helpful Hints

- It is always wise to ask permission to use something that doesn't belong to you. It doesn't matter if it is a pencil or someone's bike — ask permission!

- Sometimes, you won't get what you want. But if you have asked permission politely and correctly, you are more likely to get what you want the next time.

- Think about how you would feel if someone used something of yours without asking first. Besides feeling that the person was not polite and did not respect your property, you would be worried the item might get broken or lost.

Getting Along with Others

To be successful in dealing with people, you should:

1. **Listen** to what is being said when another person talks to you.
2. **Say something positive** if you agree with what the person said. If you don't agree, say something that won't cause an argument. Use a calm voice tone.
3. **Show interest** in what the other person has to say. Try to understand his or her point of view.

Reasons for using the skill: It is important to get along with others because you will be working and dealing with other people all your life. If you can get along with others, you are more likely to be successful in whatever you do. Getting along shows sensitivity and respect, and makes it more likely other people will behave the same way. In other words, treat others the way you want to be treated!

Helpful Hints

- Sometimes it is not easy to get along with others. If someone does something you do not like, or says something negative, you may feel like behaving the same way. Don't! Stop yourself from saying things that can hurt others' feelings. Teasing, cursing, and insults will only make matters worse. It is better to ignore others' negative behavior than to act like them.

- Getting along with others takes some effort. It is hard to understand why some people act the way they do. Try to put yourself in their place and maybe it will be easier to understand.

- If you find you don't like someone's behavior, it is better to say nothing rather than something negative.

APOLOGIZING

When you have done something that hurts another person's feelings or results in negative consequences for another person, and you need to apologize, you should:

1. **Look at the person.** It shows confidence.
2. **Say what you are sorry about.**
   (Say, *"I'm sorry I said that"* or *"I'm sorry, I didn't listen to what you said."*)
3. **Make a follow-up statement** if the person says something to you. (Say, *"Is there any way I can make it up to you?"* or *"It won't happen again."*)
4. **Thank the person for listening** (even if the person did not accept your apology).

Reasons for using the skill: It is important to apologize because it shows you are sensitive to others' feelings. It increases the chances other people will be careful of your feelings in return. Apologizing also shows you are responsible enough to admit your mistakes.

Helpful Hints

- It's easy to avoid making apologies; it takes guts to be mature enough to do it. Convince yourself that making an apology is the best thing to do and then do it!

- If the other person is upset with you, the response you receive may not be very nice at that time. Be prepared to take whatever the other person says.

- Be confident you are doing the right thing.

- When people look back on your apology, they will see you were able to realize what you did wrong. They will think about you more positively in the future.

- An apology won't erase what you did wrong. But, it may help change a person's opinion of you in the long run.

HAVING A CONVERSATION

When you are talking with someone, you should:

1. **Look at the other person.**
2. **Answer any questions the person asks,**
   and give complete answers. Just saying *"Yes"* or *"No"* usually does not give the other person enough information to keep the conversation going.
3. **Avoid negative statements.**
   Talking about past trouble you were in, bragging, calling someone names, or making other negative statements gives a bad impression.
4. **Use appropriate grammar.**
   Slang can be used with friends, but don't use it when guests or people you don't know very well are present.

5. **Start or add to conversations** by asking questions, talking about new or exciting events, or asking the other person what he or she thinks about something.

Reasons for using the skill: It is important to have good conversation skills because you can tell others what you think and get their opinions. Using this skill well makes new people you meet and guests feel more comfortable. Later in life, this skill will help you when you apply for and hold a job.

Helpful Hints

- Always include the other person's ideas in the conversation. If you don't, it won't be a conversation!

- Smile and show interest in what the other person has to say, even if you don't agree with the person.

- Keep up on current events so you have a wide range of things to talk about. People who can talk about what's happening and are good at conversation are usually well-liked and admired by other people.

GIVING COMPLIMENTS

When you want to say something nice about someone, you should:

1. **Look at the other person.**
2. **Give the compliment.**
   Tell him or her exactly what you liked.

3. **Make a follow-up statement.**
   If the person says *"Thanks,"* say *"You're welcome,"* in return.

Reasons for using the skill: Giving compliments shows you notice the accomplishments of others. People like being around someone who is pleasant, friendly, and says nice things. It also shows you have confidence in your ability to talk to others.

Helpful Hints

- Think of the exact words you want to use before you give the compliment. It will make you feel more confident and you'll be less likely to fumble around for words.

- Mean what you say. People can tell the difference between sincerity and phoniness.

- Don't overdo it. A couple of sentences will do. *("You did a good job at..."* or *"You really did well in....")*

- Smile and be enthusiastic when you give compliments. It makes the other person feel you really mean it.

ACCEPTING COMPLIMENTS

Whenever someone says something nice to you, you should:

1. **Look at the other person.**
2. **Listen** to what he or she is saying.

3. **Don't interrupt.**
4. **Say *"Thanks,"*** or something that shows you appreciate what was said.

Reasons for using the skill: Being able to accept compliments shows you can politely receive another person's positive opinion about something you have done. It also increases the chances you will receive future compliments.

Helpful Hints

- When you receive a compliment, be sure to sincerely thank the person who gave it to you. Brushing off, rejecting, or ignoring the compliment makes the other person feel uncomfortable and less likely to compliment you again.

- People give compliments for a variety of reasons. Don't waste a lot of time wondering why someone gave you a compliment. Just appreciate the fact someone took the time to say something nice to you!

LISTENING TO OTHERS

When someone is speaking, you should:

1. **Look at the person who is talking.**
2. **Sit or stand quietly.**
3. **Wait until the person is through talking.**
   Don't interrupt; it will seem like you're being rude or aren't interested in what is being said.
4. **Show that you understand.**
   Say *"Okay," "Thanks," "I see,"* etc., or ask the person to explain if you don't understand.

Reasons for using the skill: It is important to listen because it shows you are polite, pleasant, and cooperative. It increases the chances people will listen to you. And, listening well helps you do the correct thing since you are more likely to understand what the other person has said.

Helpful Hints

- If you are having trouble listening, think of how you would feel if other people didn't listen to you.

- Try to remember everything the person said. If you are going to need the information later, write it down.

- People who learn to listen well do better at their jobs and in school.

- Don't use any negative facial expressions. Continue looking at the other person, and nod your head or occasionally say something to let the other person know you are still listening.

BEING HONEST

When you have done something, whether it's good or bad, you need to be honest and always tell the truth. Being honest lets other people know they can trust you. If they can believe what you say, you will be considered trustworthy. Sometimes, people will ask you questions about your involvement in a situation. To tell the truth, you should:

1. **Look at the person.**
2. **Say exactly what happened** if you're asked to provide information.

3. **Answer any other questions.**
   These can involve what you did or did not do, or what someone else did or did not do.
4. **Don't leave out important facts.**
5. **Admit to mistakes or errors** if you made them.

Reasons for using the skill: It is important to be honest and tell the truth because people are more likely to give you a second chance if they have been able to trust you in the past. We all make mistakes, but lying will lead to more problems. If you get the reputation of being a liar, it will be hard for people to believe what you say. Plus, when you are honest, you can feel confident you have done the right thing.

Helpful Hints

- Being honest can be difficult. Many times, it will seem like lying is the easiest way out of a situation. But when people find out you have lied, the consequences are much worse.

- Lying is the opposite of telling the truth. Lying is similar to stealing or cheating. All of these behaviors will result in negative consequences for you.

SHOWING SENSITIVITY TO OTHERS

1. **Express interest and concern for others,** especially when they are having troubles.
2. Recognize that **disabled people deserve the same respect as anyone else.**

3. **Apologize or make amends** for hurting someone's feelings or causing harm.
4. Recognize that **people of different races, religions, and backgrounds deserve to be treated the same way you** would expect to be treated.

Reasons for using the skill: If you help others, they are more likely to help you. And saying you're sorry shows you can take responsibility for your actions and admit when you've done something wrong. A disability does not make a person inferior. Helping people with disabilities and treating everyone equally shows you believe that although people are different, they all deserve respect.

Helpful Hints

- If you see someone in trouble, ask if you can help.

- Sometimes, just showing you care is enough to help a person get through a difficult time.

- Be ready to help a disabled person when necessary by doing such things as holding open a door, carrying a package, or giving up your seat.

- Don't stare at disabled people or make comments about their special needs.

- You can harm someone by what you fail to do, just as easily as by what you do. Some examples are breaking a promise or not sticking up for someone who is being picked on. If you hurt someone, apologize immediately and sincerely.

- Don't make jokes or rude comments about the color of someone's skin or what he or she believes.

INTRODUCING YOURSELF

When you introduce yourself, you should:

1. **Stand up straight.**
   If you are sitting or doing something else, stop immediately, stand up, and greet the person.
2. **Look at the other person.**
3. **Offer your hand and shake hands firmly.**
   (Don't wait!)
4. **Say your name** as you are shaking hands, clearly and loudly enough to be heard easily. This shows the other person you are confident.
5. **Make a friendly statement.**
   (Say, *"Nice to meet you."*)

Reasons for using the skill: It is important to introduce yourself because it shows you are able to meet new people confidently. It makes others feel more comfortable and allows you to make a good first impression. Knowing how to introduce yourself helps you "break the ice" when meeting new people.

Helpful Hints

- Being pleasant is very important when you introduce yourself. If you are gruff or your voice is harsh, you won't leave people with a good impression. Smile when introducing yourself to the other person.

- Introductions are the first step in a conversation. If you start out on the right foot, it is more likely you will have a pleasant conversation. Make your first impression a good one.

- If the other person does not give his or her name, say *"And your name is?"*

- When you meet a person again, you will have to decide how to re-introduce yourself. If it has been a long time since you've seen the person, or if the person may have forgotten who you are, then follow the same steps as in this skill. If the time in between was short, you may choose just to say, *"Hi, in case you forgot, I'm...."*

- Try to remember the other person's name. Other people will be impressed when you take the time to remember them.

Chapter 13

Making Decisions and Solving Problems

N o matter how old they are, children are making decisions all the time.

A strange man in the park asks a 6-year-old girl to help him look for his puppy. What does she do?

A 10-year-old's friend tries to get him to steal things at a store. What does he do?

A 16-year-old is pressured by her boyfriend to "make out" at a party. What does she do?

In each situation, these kids have a choice to make. Children frequently make decisions on the spur of the moment, sometimes without thinking. They tend to look at solutions to problems as being black or white, all or nothing, yes or no, do it or don't do it. Children also focus on the immediate situation and have difficulty looking beyond it to see how a decision could affect them later.

As a parent, how can you prepare your children to make the best decisions?

The SODAS Method

We've learned children are more likely to make good choices when they have a structured way to look at a problem and its possible solutions. The problem-solving method we help parents to teach their kids is called **SODAS®**. **SODAS** stands for:

S = **S**ituation

O = **O**ptions

D = **D**isadvantages

A = **A**dvantages

S = **S**olution

The **SODAS** method helps both children and adults think more clearly and make decisions based on sound reasoning. The principles are simple, and the method can be adapted to many situations.

The two main goals of using **SODAS** are:

- To give **parents and children a process for solving problems and making decisions together.**

- To help **parents teach children how to solve problems and make decisions on their own.**

Let's look at each step of the **SODAS** process.

Define the Situation

Before you can solve a problem, you need to know what the problem is. Defining the situation sometimes takes the greatest amount of time because children often use vague or emotional descriptions. Also, children aren't always aware that a certain situation could cause problems. A young child may think running into the street to retrieve his soccer ball isn't a problem; he's only thinking about getting the ball back. He doesn't realize going after the ball is dangerous.

Other decisions may not involve obvious dangers, but they still may have drawbacks that children have to consider when making a choice. Children will have to decide how to spend their allowance, what kids to hang around with, or whether to go out for sports or get a job. They can quickly run through the **SODAS** process to make these daily decisions.

Tips for helping children define a situation:

- Ask specific, open-ended questions. Avoid asking questions your child can answer with a one-word answer: *"Yes," "No," "Fine," "Good,"* etc. Instead, ask questions such as, *"What did you do then?"* or *"What happened after you said that?"* These questions help you piece together what is happening or what really occurred.

- Teach children to focus on the entire situation, not just part of it. For example, questions that identify who, what, when, and where will help you and your child come up with a clear picture of the whole situation.

- Summarize the information. Children sometimes get so overwhelmed by the emotions surrounding a situation that they lose sight of what the actual problem is. State the problem in its simplest, most specific form. Ask your child if your summary of the situation is correct.

Here is an example of how a parent helped her child define a problem with a bully at school.

Mom:	*"Keenan, tell me what you were doing before the fight started between you and Mike at school today."*
Keenan:	*"I walked into the bathroom and Mike started messing with me."*
Mom:	*"What exactly did Mike say or do when you walked into the bathroom?"*
Keenan:	*"He started making fun of me and calling me names in front of some other guys."*
Mom:	*"How did that make you feel?"*
Keenan:	*"It wasn't a big deal at first, but he kept going. That's when I started getting really mad."*
Mom:	*"Okay, what did you do next?"*
Keenan:	*"I asked him to knock it off. He kept it up and pushed me into one of the stalls. I pushed him back. That's when a teacher came into the bathroom and broke it all up."*
Mom:	*"Sounds like you and Mike are having problems getting along."*

Come Up with Options

Once you have a complete description of the situation, you can begin discussing options — the choices your child has for solving the problem. There usually are several options for every problem. Unfortunately, children frequently think of solutions as "all or nothing." For example, a student who gets a bad grade on a test immediately wants to change classes because everything is "ruined." Or, if a bully is picking on another kid, your child may think the only solution is to gang up on the bully. It's common for children to only see one solution to a problem, or take the first one that pops into their heads. Other times, they may see no options at all.

Your role as a parent is to get your child to think. Ask questions like, *"Can you think of anything else you could do?"* or *"What else could solve the problem?"* Consistently asking these questions helps your child learn a process for making decisions without your guidance.

Tips for identifying options:

- Let your child list good and bad options. Many times, parents want to cut right to the chase and tell children what to do. But the purpose here is to get your child to think of ways to make a decision on his or her own.

- Limit options to no more than three. Any more tends to get confusing. (Also, make sure at least one of the options is reasonable and has a chance for success.)

- Suggest options if your child is having trouble coming up with them. This way, he or she learns there is more than one option in many situations.

Let's continue with the example we started earlier with Keenan and the bully at school.

Mom:	*"Keenan, what are some other more positive ways you can handle this situation in the future?"*
Keenan:	*"I don't know. I'm sick of Mike messing with me."*
Mom:	*"Fighting won't solve anything and it will only lead to trouble, so let's come up with some better options."*
Keenan:	*"Well, I suppose I could just walk away when he starts messing with me."*
Mom:	*"That's a great option! Can you think of any others?"*
Keenan:	*"I could stay away from Mike for a few days."*
Mom:	*"Good. What about help from a teacher?"*
Keenan:	*"Yeah. If it gets bad enough, I could go talk to the coach. He's cool."*
Mom:	*"Those are all good options."*

Think of Disadvantages and Advantages for Each Option

In these steps, you and your child discuss the pros and cons of each option. This helps your child see the connection between each option and what could happen if that option is chosen.

Tips for reviewing disadvantages and advantages:

- Ask your child for his or her thoughts about each option. What's good about the option? What's bad about the option? Why would the option work? Why wouldn't the option work?

- Help your child come up with both disadvantages and advantages for every option. This will be easier for your child to do with certain options; he or she may not have the experience or knowledge to know possible outcomes for all options.

Let's continue with Keenan and options for his problem.

Mom: *"Okay, let's go over the advantages and disadvantages of the three options we came up with."*

Mom and Keenan write down and discuss the pros and cons for each option: 1) walking away; 2) avoiding the places where Mike and the other bullies hang out; and 3) getting help from his coach.

Choose a Solution

At this point, it is time to choose an option that would work best. Briefly summarize the disadvantages and advantages for each option and ask your child to choose the best one.

Tips for choosing a solution:

- Make sure your child knows the options and the possible outcomes of each one. You're trying to help your child make an informed decision and establish a pattern for making future decisions.

- Some decisions are hard to make. If the decision doesn't need to be made immediately, let your child think about it for a while.

247

Here's how Keenan and Mom came up with a solution.

Mom: *"Keenan, we've gone over all the advantages and disadvantages of each option. Now you'll need to decide what option you want to use to try to solve this problem. I will give you some time to think about it. Let's talk after dinner."*

Keenan: (after dinner) *"I think the best thing to do is to just avoid Mike for a while. If he starts up again, I'll just walk away and talk to you about it again."*

Mom: *"That's a great solution! Remember, if you find yourself getting mad or scared, you can always go talk to your coach."*

Helpful Hints

Parents usually have a lot of questions about **SODAS** and the types of situations in which it can be used. Here are some things to think about when using the **SODAS** method.

Sometimes, children pick options that don't sit too well with their parents. In general, if the decisions won't hurt anyone, and aren't illegal or contrary to your moral or religious beliefs, then let your child make the choice and learn from his or her decision. For example, your son might insist he wants to spend most of his money on a very expensive video game. You may not agree with his choice, but it won't affect anyone but him (and his cash flow) if he decides to buy the game. You could let him buy it and learn from the consequences. Perhaps he will enjoy the game so much he won't mind not having money for other activities. On the other hand, he might wish later he had not bought such an expensive game. We suggest you let your son know that if he wants money after he spends all of his, you will not give it to him. If he wants to work or do something to earn money, that's a different story. But don't let him off the hook by giving in to his pleas for money. This is one way he'll learn to make good decisions about spending his money.

Occasionally, children think of options or want to make decisions that are illegal, immoral, or harmful to them or others. If this happens with your child, you should clearly and firmly state your disapproval, spell out the disadvantages to that solution, and let your child know the consequences of making that choice. For example, if your 16-year-old daughter decides she wants to drink alcohol when she's out with her friends, you can let her know you won't tolerate her drinking and spell out all of the many dangers. Also, tell her what consequences she will earn if she decides to drink. Sometimes, despite all of our efforts, children still make wrong choices or decisions. When that occurs, you must follow through with the consequences you described. Then, help your child go through the **SODAS** process and come up with more acceptable solutions.

While you should encourage your children to make some decisions on their own, you need to let them know you are there to help at any time. This includes supporting them as they implement the solution. If a solution does not work out the way your child planned, offer support and empathy. You and your child can then return to the **SODAS** format to find another solution to the problem.

In situations where you think it will be helpful, have your child practice trying out the solution. Practice builds up your child's confidence about trying the solution he or she has chosen and improves the chances for success.

Finally, check with your child to see how the solution worked. Set a specific time to talk about this. This is an excellent opportunity for you to praise your child for following through with his or her decision. You also can look for additional solutions, if necessary.

Summary

If this type of problem-solving is new to you, begin with a small problem first. Give your kids time to get comfortable with the process. Many kids don't have the patience to think things out. They can get frustrated and "just want to get it over with." Don't let them make rash choices. Teach them to make good decisions.

SODAS is an excellent process for teaching your child how to make decisions. It is practical and can be applied to many different situations your child may face. You can feel confident you have given your child an effective, easy-to-use method for solving problems.

☞ CHAPTER REVIEW

What is the SODAS method?

A process for helping parents and children solve problems and make decisions together.

When should parents use the SODAS method with their children?

SODAS can be used for almost any problem children face. It should not be used with issues that are clearly illegal, immoral, or harmful to the child or others, but it can be used to help teach morals and values. **SODAS** can be used with any problem parents are willing to let their children try to solve.

What does SODAS stand for?

S = **S**ituation

O = **O**ptions

D = **D**isadvantages

A = **A**dvantages

S = **S**olution

☆ ACTION PLAN

1. Take some time to answer the following questions:

   - What is the most important thing you learned in this chapter?

   - What do you plan to do differently as a result of what you've learned?

2. Become more familiar with **SODAS** by going through the problem-solving process using an issue you are facing (for example, how to deal with an unpleasant co-worker, how to meet your budget while increasing your savings, whether or not to approach your neighbor about his barking dog, etc.). Using a pencil and paper, describe the situation, think of several options, list the advantages and disadvantages of each option, and choose a solution.

Next, watch for an opportunity to go through **SODAS** with your child. He or she may tell you about a problem that is occurring at school or with a friend, or may need to make a choice between two different activities. Or, perhaps you want to talk with your children about what to do on your summer vacation. Whatever it is, the next time your child must make a significant choice or decision, use the opportunity to teach him or her the **SODAS** method of problem solving.

Q&A
FOR PARENTS

Q **Am I supposed to allow my children to make decisions on everything?**

A It's very important you teach your children how to go about making good decisions and to give them plenty of opportunities to practice using the **SODAS** method. However, you still have the right to tell your children which issues they can work out on their own, which ones you will assist them with, and which issues you will decide.

Q **My son already has good judgment. Do I still need to use the SODAS method with him?**

A Why not? Your son needs concrete tools and strategies to help him get through life. Teaching him the **SODAS** method will give him another tool to successfully go about solving problems. Also, you can use **SODAS** to share with him your values, morals, and views on various subjects without it sounding like a lecture.

Q **Is my 6-year-old child too young for the SODAS method?**

A Absolutely not! But with young children, it's usually a good idea to keep the process and the number of options short and simple. Introducing **SODAS** to young children can help them become better decision-makers as they get older.

Chapter 14
Holding Family Meetings

etween work, school, sports, organizations, and other activities, it's sometimes hard for parents and children to get together to make plans, share information, or just talk. Family Meetings are a way for family members to find time in their busy day to spend time together and work and have fun as a group.

When you make Family Meetings part of your daily or weekly routine, everyone has an opportunity to be involved in the day-to-day workings of the family and to have a voice in what the family does and plans to do. Beginning the tradition of having Family Meetings also creates a way to share and pass on important family values to future generations.

There are four main reasons for having Family Meetings:

1. Family members can praise and encourage each other and let everyone know about individual and group achievements.

The Family Meeting is an ideal time to praise each of your children and to let everyone know about achievements or accomplishments. Show your approval for improvements at school, for offers to help out around the house, or for getting along with another child. Let everyone know about attempts your kids have made to solve problems. Think of creative ways for your children to learn to praise one another. They also can show their appreciation of you by saying *"Thanks."* One parent we know starts each meeting by having everyone say something nice about the person sitting to his or her right. This is a positive way to get the meeting started.

2. A family can coordinate schedules for the week and make plans to pick up necessary supplies, provide transportation, and get to upcoming appointments or meetings.

Your kids can tell you about their upcoming activities, and make plans for school or for playing with friends. You can remind your children or your spouse about doctor and dentist appointments, school conferences, or other obligations. You also can ask important questions, like who needs supplies, transportation, money, or materials for the week. A home operates better when family members share information like this. It certainly makes life easier for you when plans are made in advance.

3. A family can have discussions about what's happening.

Here's a time for you and your children to share information about all those other "things" going on in your lives. Give them a chance to talk about what happened at school, what they discussed in class about local or world events, problems they're having with friends, and things they'd like to do as a family. You then get to share your opinion about these important issues. Be sure to bring some of your own "things" to discuss, like what you've been doing at work, current events, what's happening with relatives, and your opinions of the latest fads or music. A Family Meeting is a time to talk and listen, to share and discuss. This opportunity helps children develop their own views and beliefs by listening to the opinions of others. It can be fun, entertaining, and educational as it brings the family closer together.

4. A family can make decisions as a group.

You can use the Family Meeting as the place where your children share in making routine decisions. These could include deciding what the next week's menus should be, where to go on a family outing, which TV show to watch, or how household chores should be split up. Children will be much happier if they have a chance to give their input when decisions are made. But give them some limits to work within. For example, if your family wants to go to a movie for your family outing, you could say, "Kids, the first thing you need to decide is what night we should go out. Then, pick a G- or PG-rated movie that all of us will like." This way, your children get to make some decisions within the limits you set. They may get to choose what night to go out and what movie to see, but they don't get the choice of selecting an R-rated movie. That is a limit you set. You should always make major decisions, or decisions of a moral or legal nature. Another good, easy example of a family decision might be what church service to attend.

Family Meeting Steps

Family Meetings can be held anytime, but they should be scheduled so all family members can attend. This might mean having meetings right after dinner or on Saturday mornings before breakfast. Meetings can be held regularly (daily or weekly), and special meetings can be called when it is necessary to discuss something unexpected or an issue or decision that needs to be addressed immediately.

Here are the steps for having a Family Meeting and an explanation of each:

1. **Call the meeting to order at the scheduled time.**
2. **Thank family members for attending the meeting.**
3. **Make announcements and coordinate family schedules as needed.**
4. **Review and vote on any old business.**
5. **Discuss any new family concerns and make necessary decisions.**
6. **Praise individuals for achievements and close the meeting.**

STEP 1: Call the meeting to order at the scheduled time.

Try having Family Meetings at the same regular time. This creates consistency and structure. Family members will begin to expect and look forward to Family Meetings as part of their weekly or daily routines.

Be sure to start the meeting with encouragement and something fun that gets everyone involved. Depending on how close to a meal you schedule your meeting, having snacks during or right after the meeting might be a good way to motivate participation. You also could use privileges or treats to reward being on time. Younger children can earn stickers or stars they can put on a reward chart.

The beginning of a Family Meeting is also a good time to use Preventive Teaching to head off any problems that might have occurred in the past. You can use Preventive Teaching to prepare your children to discuss a new topic or issue or one they don't know much about. For example, Dad might say something like this:

> *"Before we start our meeting, I want to remind everyone not to speak out of turn. You should speak only when the person who is leading the meeting calls on you by saying it's your turn to speak. Now, I'd like everyone to be quiet and pay attention to Mom while she goes over what we decided at our last Family Meeting."*

STEP 2: Thank family members for attending the meeting.

Always thank individual family members for taking time to attend the meeting. This also is a great time to use Effective Praise to recognize family members for being on time and participating. For example, you could say something like this:

> *"Great job everyone for coming to the Family Meeting and being on time. When everyone's on time, we get done sooner and you can get back to doing what you want. Way to go!"*

STEP 3: Make announcements and coordinate family schedules as needed.

Anytime you can get all or most of your family together in one place, it is a good opportunity to make necessary

259

announcements or to inform your family of important changes in routines. Also, remind family members to bring news about their sports, extracurricular activities, and work schedules, and to mention any special outings or appointments so that rides, supervision, and household routines can be arranged accordingly.

STEP 4: Review and vote on any old business.

If there are any concerns or decisions that need to be reviewed or voted on, make sure you revisit those issues and come to a final decision, if possible.

STEP 5: Discuss any new family concerns and make necessary decisions.

Family Meetings are a perfect time to discuss anything that affects the family. For example, you might need to decide where to go for vacation or to adjust curfews and bedtimes for summer. The list of Family Meeting topics and agendas is almost limitless.

STEP 6: Praise individuals for achievements and close the meeting.

Family Meetings should always end on a positive note. Some families conduct "round robin" praise, where everyone takes a turn praising others at the meeting. When everyone who's earned praise receives it, Mom or Dad can close the meeting. This is a great time to announce achievements or praise improvements of family members. Remember: Praise is the most effective way to get your children to be interested and participate in Family Meetings.

Dealing with Disruptions

During a meeting, each person should be given a chance to voice his or her opinion after being recognized by the person who is leading the meeting. Everyone should have the opportunity to speak without being interrupted. Anyone who speaks out of turn, or displays other inappropriate behavior that disrupts the meeting, should be disciplined immediately using Corrective Teaching.

For example, if your daughter starts talking while her brother tells the family about his day at school, you could say something like this to her:

"Alicia, right now you are interrupting by speaking out of turn. You've lost 15 minutes of watching your favorite show tonight. You should wait your turn to speak and speak only when the leader has recognized you. Then you can say what you want to say without losing any privileges. You've done a good job of listening so far and haven't interrupted me. Good job! Now, if you raise your hand and wait your turn to speak during the rest of the meeting, you may earn back some of the TV time you lost."

Sometimes, when decisions need to be made during Family Meetings, tempers can flare and emotions can get out of control. In these situations, you may need to use Teaching Self-Control to get things calmed down so the meeting can continue.

For example, if one of your children loses self-control during a meeting, you could say something like this:

"Right now you are yelling and calling people names. Please use your Staying Calm Plan to calm down.

We'll take a break from our meeting to give you some time to do that."

Once the child has calmed down, you could continue by saying:

"Are you calm enough to control your emotions while we talk? (The child nods his head.) Good. I want you to listen to me without interrupting. Next time you feel upset about something we're discussing at our Family Meeting, ask if you can take a break. Then ask to go to your room so you can take a few deep breaths before using your Staying Calm Plan. Let's try that now. (Child complies.) Now let's pretend someone has just said something that made you mad. Take a deep breath and ask to take a break in your room. (Child complies.) Great job of practicing with me. Because you lost self-control at the Family Meeting tonight, you've lost your snack and will have to clean up the kitchen tonight."

Helpful Hints

Schedule Family Meetings at a convenient time for all or most family members.

Meetings can occur every day, once a week, or even every other week, depending on your family's need to spend time together and the amount of family business. Make sure you choose the most opportune time for the family. Be flexible. This could mean having a meeting on Saturday morning or on Sunday night after dinner. Some families choose to have Family Meetings after dinner every night. Other families don't make a schedule; they have meetings whenever everyone is home. Adjust the time of your meetings to fit your needs. It's more important that you have a meeting where everyone can participate than to strictly follow a meeting schedule no matter who can or cannot attend.

Be creative when schedules conflict.

For example, you can have a conference call or social media online meeting when a family member is out of town on meeting night.

Make Family Meetings fun.

Everyone learns more when they like or are interested in what they are being taught. Don't make your meetings all work and no play; that makes it dull for everyone. Variety is an important element in keeping kids interested and the novelty of the meeting fresh. There will be times when you may have to make a serious decision or discuss difficult issues, but these should occur infrequently. Most of the time, you should concentrate on sharing information or recognizing the good things family members are doing.

Emphasize the use of social skills at Family Meetings.

Encourage your children's attempts to use skills (like listening, or giving or accepting compliments), and their achievements and improvements as they learn when and how to use them in different situations.

Keep Family Meetings short.

Meetings should last no longer than 15 to 20 minutes. Keep topics simple enough so everyone can understand and discuss them, and so problems can be resolved easily. As your children improve their skills and as they get older, you may be able to have slightly longer meetings and take on bigger issues.

One way to keep meetings moving is to use a "talking stick" and timer. These are helpful if family members have difficulty being brief or staying on task. A talking stick is a colorfully decorated stick a family member picks up when it is his or her turn to talk, make a motion, or share a concern. Only the person holding the stick can speak and everyone else must listen and be quiet until it is his or her turn. A timer can be used to control the amount of time a family member can speak.

Use Preventive Teaching.

Before a meeting, teach your children how to appropriately bring up topics for discussion and have them practice how to give opinions without offending others. Also, help them practice how to compliment others without sounding corny or insincere. And, teach them how to give and accept criticism without overreacting. This is a perfect time to teach your children what to say and how to say it.

Keep a written record of decisions, schedules, issues, and so on.

Use a notebook to record Family Meeting notes and display a summary of the notes in a convenient, well-visited spot. Many parents choose to post schedules or announcements on the refrigerator. Keeping records and putting notes where all family members can see them cuts down on confusion and keeps everyone informed.

Give everyone a chance to speak.

You can teach cooperation, respect, and sensitivity by ensuring everyone, from the youngest to oldest, has a voice in the way your family operates.

Give positive consequences.

Give rewards and praise for listening to others, for not interrupting, for bringing up good suggestions, and for offering to help out. Family Meetings are an ideal time to praise your children.

Use all of your teaching skills during Family Meetings.

For example:

- If one of your children receives minor criticism and begins to argue and make excuses, use Corrective Teaching.

- If your child doesn't respond to Corrective Teaching, use Teaching Self-Control.

- Use Preventive Teaching before bringing up a sensitive issue or if it's hard for your child to express opinions in front of others.

- Use the **SODAS** method to solve problems.

Using SODAS at Family Meetings

In Chapter 13, we discussed the **SODAS** method for solving problems and making decisions. In addition to teaching this method to your children so they can learn to solve problems independently, you can use it at Family Meetings to teach them how to solve problems and make good decisions as a group and as a member of a group.

Let's look at an example of how **SODAS** can be used at a Family Meeting.

The family has just finished dinner and is sitting at the dinner table.

Dad:	*"Okay everyone, hang on for a moment. Let's have a short Family Meeting. Your Mom and I have decided that for the yard work you did today, you've earned either watching one movie on pay-per-view tonight or going swimming this weekend. We don't want a big argument over which one you want to do, so let's do a quick SODAS."*
Mom:	(Situation) *"You all have done a great job participating at Family Meetings lately! Keep it up tonight and we can make this short and sweet so you can get back to doing things you like. Does everyone understand the decision you have to make? You can either choose and watch a movie tonight or go swimming this weekend."*
Joey:	*"Swimming! I wanna go to the pool!"* (Joey stands up and starts hopping around the room.)
Mom:	*"Joey, I know you're excited but you're interrupting the Family Meeting. Please sit down. For interrupting, you'll pick an item out of the Job Jar and do it to-night.* (Joey sits down and says, *"Okay."*) *For the rest of the meet-ing, remember to raise your hand if you want to talk."*

Dad: *"Remember to stay calm and be considerate of each other when making your decision. What can you say or do to be more considerate toward each other?"*

Samantha: *"Think about how the solution might be best for everyone in the family and not just one person."*

Joey: *"Listen to the other person."*

Brendan: *"Don't say negative things if you don't like what someone says."*

Mom: *"Wow! Those are all great ways to be considerate. Nice job! Now, let's look at the advantages and disadvantages of going swimming or getting a video."*

Brendan: (Disadvantage) *"I've already made plans this weekend to go to a baseball game with Emily. So I guess you can count me out on Saturday."*

Dad: *"It's a family activity and everyone should be allowed to take part in it."*

Samantha: (New Option) *"What if we let Brendan pick out a movie for tonight and we go swimming this weekend without him? Then, he could still go to the game with Emily."*

Mom: *"What do you think about that Brendan?"*

Brendan: (Disadvantage) *"That's okay with me. But do I have to pick a kiddy movie so Joey can watch it?"*

Dad: (Advantage) *"There are lots of good movies out there we can all watch together. Let's get on the pay-per-view menu for a few minutes and see what we can find."*

(Everyone agrees and heads off to look for a movie. After some discussion, Brendan selects a movie.)

Mom: (Solution) *"So, do we all agree?* (Everyone says, *"Yes."*) *Great. So here's your decision: Tonight we'll watch the movie Brendan picked out and on Saturday the rest of us will go swimming while he spends time with Emily."*

Dad: *"Nice job, guys! You all really worked well together to find a good solution and you took everyone's needs into consideration. For your hard work, let's have some ice cream for dessert!"*

Summary

Family Meetings can be some of the most important times your family spends together. You'll improve communication among family members and your children will feel like they have a voice in family matters. They also will gain confidence in their ability to share opinions and accept compliments and criticism. And everyone will be better informed about what's going on in each other's lives — at work, at school, with friends, and at home.

Another important component of Family Meetings is making decisions. When children and parents can work together to solve problems and make decisions, things get done and everyone is happier. The **SODAS** method is an effective way for families to work together to identify a situation, explore options, discuss the advantages and disadvantages of each option, and come to a solution that will benefit everyone.

☞ CHAPTER REVIEW

What are four main reasons for having Family Meetings?

1. Family members can praise and encourage each other and let everyone know about individual and group achievements.

2. A family can coordinate schedules for the week and make plans to pick up necessary supplies, provide transportation, and get to upcoming events.

3. A family can have discussions about what's happening in the family (rule changes), in a family member's life (school issues), and/or in the world (current events).

4. A family can make decisions as a group.

☆ ACTION PLAN

1. Take some time to answer the following questions:

   - What is the most important thing you learned in this chapter?

   - What do you plan to do differently as a result of what you've learned?

2. Take a few minutes to plan the agenda for a Family Meeting. If you have never held one before, plan a short agenda focusing on no more than two topics. The first could be a discussion of what you and your children want your Family Meetings to be and what rules should apply to your meetings. Bring a few simple rules to the meeting yourself — for example, family members should not interrupt each other. Let your children participate in the discussion about any additional rules.

   Your agenda also should include an enjoyable topic or fun activity. You could, for example, plan to discuss an upcoming vacation, outing, or birthday, or recognize one of your children for an academic or athletic accomplishment. It's important to make your first Family Meeting a positive experience for your children so they will look forward to and cooperate during future meetings.

Q&A

FOR PARENTS

Q What if my kids don't want to participate in Family Meetings?

A Don't give up on having Family Meetings! Instead, start off by keeping your meetings upbeat, positive, and brief. Include topics that will interest your kids. Also, try to make the meetings fun without getting off task. Your kids will eventually come around and look forward to the time you spend together.

Q I'm a single parent with one child. How can I avoid getting into arguments with my child at a Family Meeting?

A For the most part, your Family Meeting will run the same way that it would for families with more than one child. Obviously, there will be much less discussion. If you find that you can't come to an understanding with your child, table the matter for another time. It is often a balancing act for single parents when they try to give their child an opportunity to share his or her thoughts and make decisions. Remember not to fall into the traps of either debating every little thing or making all the decisions yourself because it's what you want or think is best.

Q How many topics should be discussed at a Family Meeting?

A Sticking to one or two topics for each meeting is a good rule of thumb. If you have a complex issue to discuss, you may need more than one Family Meeting to break it down and arrive at a decision. Always work to keep meetings short but fruitful.

Q Should I give my children some responsibility in running the Family Meeting?

A Absolutely! In some families, older children who have shown they are capable can run the meeting — with your help of course. Also, you might have a younger child keep track of what the family discusses in a notebook. Doing things to give your children responsibility during Family Meetings creates a sense of ownership and makes it more likely they will cooperate during the meeting and follow through with decisions that are made.

Chapter 15
Establishing Family Routines and Traditions

> haring experiences, spending time together, and celebrating important events are a big part of what helps make families strong and family life happy. Unfortunately, these things don't always happen naturally. Parents and children have to work at creating a home environment that fosters a spirit of cooperation and where both the common and special events of everyday life are meaningful and enjoyable.

In this chapter, we'll discuss the importance of establishing family routines and family traditions as ways to bring family members together so everyone feels a sense of caring, respect, responsibility, and belonging.

What Is a Family Routine?

We define a routine as a custom, habit, schedule, or practice of a family. Routines can set a positive tone in your home where tasks get done, family members share news and information, and, most importantly, parents and kids spend time together. They can serve a wide variety of purposes, from reinforcing a family value like "waste not, want not" by emptying the refrigerator every Friday night for a potluck supper of leftovers, to stressing the importance of education with a nightly mandatory study time. Routines like attending weekly church services together as a family could also be discussed at Family Meetings (see Chapter 14).

A routine also is a helpful tool that lets children know how important they are and how they fit into the family. It can tell them other people count on them and their abilities. A simple routine can teach a child important life lessons like respect for self, consideration of others, accomplishing goals, and overcoming challenges.

A family routine can be as structured or as flexible as you want, but it should be something your family can manage and maintain. In other words, it should fit your family's lifestyle and schedules. This means setting reasonable goals and guidelines for things like doing chores, having Family Meetings, having a "family night," religious practices, or making a decision. For example, avoid making grandiose plans for getting all the chores done before school if your kids have problems with getting up early enough to do them. Don't develop a routine that calls for a Family Meeting on a specific day and time if your work hours or those of your teenager might change and create a conflict. Remember, a routine should be a good fit for your family. Just because your best friend or neighbor has a strict rule for having dinner at precisely 6 p.m. doesn't mean the same schedule will work for you.

One of the most important things to remember as a parent when it comes to a family routine is that it will change. As your children grow, your family's needs and lifestyle will change and your routines will require adjustments. Changes in a routine can occur slowly over time, or they may come in rapid-fire succession, depending on the circumstances and the family. Whether your family is in constant motion or putters at a snail's pace, it is your job as a parent to be flexible and recognize when changes are necessary. Change doesn't have to mean chaos. You can maintain consistency and continue to meet the overall expectations of your routines by simply sharing with your kids and other family members what will be done differently and why. What should remain the same is a routine that teaches and reinforces a family's values, a positive style of living, and the ability to spend time and get along with each other.

Why Parents Should Establish Family Routines

Having routines makes perfect sense, especially if they help your child behave better at home and perform better at school. For example, if your child has consistent routines for studying, bedtime, and starting the day, he or she will probably be better prepared for school. Children need structure in their lives, and routines help provide that. Routines also help parents. By setting expectations, schedules, rules, and specific ways of doing things ahead of time, as part of a daily or weekly routine, you will spend less time reminding your children about what they are supposed to do or not do. Your children will begin to understand your expectations and their responsibilities as members of the family, and will begin to act on their own to fulfill those responsibilities, without being constantly reminded. Your children also will be more successful in starting new routines and changing old ones when they are a part of the decision-making process and are learning the skills they need to carry out tasks and chores.

Creating a Family Routine

There aren't any real steps for setting up family routines because every family is different. But here are some guidelines you might find helpful:

1. First, make sure your child knows the appropriate social skills for carrying out a routine.

A routine can sometimes be too complex or even too simple for children, depending on their social and developmental ability. A young child may simply need to learn to follow instructions before you make a chore a routine part of his or her daily activity. An older child who has shown he or she can follow instructions should be able to take on a chore routine with some simple guidelines or reminders.

2. Address children's negative or inappropriate behavior right away.

If you find yourself repeatedly having to follow up with your child because he or she is constantly breaking routine rules or ignoring a schedule, the problem might not be with the routine but with your child. Some children who have the necessary skills to do what is being asked still might refuse to follow instructions out of defiance or stubbornness. When children have difficulties obeying rules or following guidelines, parents should immediately correct those behaviors and teach appropriate behaviors and skills. (See Chapter 10, "Correcting Misbehavior.")

Teaching a few simple social skills and correcting your child when he or she has difficulty following through on a routine can make all the difference, and can help you and your child achieve your goals.

3. Set reasonable expectations.

Ask yourself the following questions:

- Have I **taught** my child how to do this routine?
- Have I **modeled** these expectations to my child?
- Is my **child developmentally ready** to do what I am asking?
- Has my child been **able to show me** he or she can do what I ask?

If your answers to these questions are "Yes," your child should be able to meet your expectations.

4. Use charts and contracts to motivate your children to follow routines and to measure their progress.

Charts are excellent visual tools for helping kids and parents keep track of what they're doing well and what needs improvement. Contracts are great for getting older children to agree to cooperate with a new family routine or with changes in a routine. (See Chapter 8, "Reaching Goals Using Charts and Contracts.")

Be sure to get your children's input on a contract or chart before changing or adding a routine to your family's schedule. Children are more likely and willing to follow through on a routine if they helped create it and have some ownership.

Also, change your perspective of your family's success. That is, decide what criteria you expect your family — especially your children — to meet in order to consider a task or an activity a success.

5. Acknowledge, encourage, and reward cooperation and accomplishments.

Children like to be noticed when they show responsibility or work well with others. When your kids (or the whole family) have done a good job of sticking with a routine, schedules, and planned activities, acknowledge their efforts, encourage their attempts, and reward cooperation.

6. Use a variety of motivators to get children involved.

Consequences that are given as rewards for following rules and schedules work better when there are many to choose from. If you notice that a routine isn't working as well as it once did, you may want to check with your kids to see if they are still motivated by the consequences you are using. Routinely changing consequences can keep kids interested in following a routine.

7. Review routines during Family Meetings.

Family Meetings are a good time to check schedules, activities, and the family's general lifestyle to see if there have been changes and to look at possible revisions. Review your family routines frequently at Family Meetings to make sure everyone is still on track and to discuss temporary changes in routines such as the special events or practices related to an upcoming religious holiday.

Teaching Social Skills for Routines

There are some very important social skills every child should learn as part of establishing family routines. These skills enable children to understand, participate, and be successful when it comes to meeting the expectations and responsibilities that come with routines. These skills are:

- Following Instructions
- Accepting Criticism or a Consequence
- Asking for Help
- Showing Consideration for Others
- Accepting Responsibility

Here is an example of how a mom could teach her 9-year-old son to follow instructions using the parenting skill of Preventive Teaching before starting him on a new bedtime routine.

Mom: *"Jason, summer is almost over and school starts in two weeks. That means you will have to go back to a bedtime routine where you'll have to go to bed earlier. Before we change over to the new bedtime schedule, I want you to work on following my instructions so you will have fewer problems going to bed early. When I give you an instruction, you should look at me, say 'Okay' to show you heard the instruction, do what is asked immediately, and, if necessary, check back with me when you are done. When you follow instructions like this, it shows me you are growing up and may be ready for a later bedtime. Do you understand? Let's practice this three times before bedtime*

> *tonight. Right now, please go lay your*
> *pajamas out on your bed and come*
> *and let me know when you're done.*
> (Jason does what his mother asked.)
> *Great job of following instructions!"*

If Mom continues this teaching through the two weeks prior to changing the bedtime routine, Jason is more likely to follow her new instruction to go to bed earlier. At the same time, Mom will be able to determine how well Jason can follow instructions. If he is doing well, she may consider rewarding his efforts with a later bedtime on the weekends. Remember what we said earlier about change being dependent on the family members and the circumstances? This is a good example of one of those situations where changing a routine makes a lot of sense.

Which Social Skill to Teach?

Read the following situations and decide what social skill the child needs to learn to successfully follow the family routine. The answers are in a key at the end of the list.

1. James has difficulty finishing homework during study time at home. He often leaves the room, complains his work is too hard, and makes several trips to the bathroom. It sometimes takes him hours to complete one assignment. What social skill does James need to learn so study time goes smoother?

2. Michaela gets her chores done quickly in the morning. But, when anyone tells her the chore wasn't done correctly, she argues, pouts, and

generally throws a fit. What social skill does Michaela need to learn so she can get her chores done and redo them, if necessary, without arguing?

3.   Tanya mumbles and looks puzzled as she struggles to complete her math homework. What skill does Tanya need to learn in order to be more productive during study time?

4.   Tommy always wants his mom to help him pick up the many toys he scatters around his room as he plays each day. If she tells him to do the chore himself, he whines and cries until she finally helps him. Mom feels Tommy can clean up after himself. What skill does Mom need to teach Tommy so he can take on the task alone?

5.   Mom likes to get up early on Saturday morning to dust, vacuum, and mop floors. Her kids would rather sleep in on Saturdays than get up and help. What social skill could Mom teach her kids so they will get up earlier and help her?

Answer Key: 1) Following Instructions; 2) Accepting Criticism; 3) Asking for Help; 4) Staying Calm; 5) Volunteering

What Is a Family Tradition?

Traditions are an important part of family life that help define families and give them unique identities. **Traditions are the rules, routines, celebrations, and habits that make each family special.** The traditions you create with your children will leave them with wonderful memories and help bring everyone in your home together.

Family traditions can take on many different forms. Holiday celebrations are the most common type of family tradition. Here are some examples of ways to celebrate cultural, national, or spiritual holidays:

- Have a family meazr, or do some other community service project.

- Talk to your children about your family's ethnic, cultural, or religious heritage during holidays like Cinco de Mayo, Kwanzaa, St. Patrick's Day, Hanukkah, Easter, Thanksgiving, Christmas, and others.

Besides holidays, there are many other events that lend themselves to celebrations and traditions that you can start with your children and pass on to them when they start families of their own. Birthdays, anniversaries, graduations, family reunions, and special accomplishments or achievements all can be celebrated with parties, special dinners, and gatherings of relatives and friends. And each of these special celebrations can include old and new traditions. For example, at a birthday party, the person who is celebrating a birthday gets to choose a special food for dinner or a special dessert. Everyone can look at the birthday person's baby pictures or pictures taken when he or she was younger. One family we know of has the unusual tradition of sneaking up on the birthday person during the party and putting butter on his or her nose. This family has been doing this for so long, no one remembers just how it got started, but it's always a fun moment for everyone.

Routines as Traditions

Traditions don't always have to be tied to special events. Any regular routine that gives a family identity and helps everyone get through the day can be considered a family tradition. (These can include things like Sunday dinners with the grandparents, a piggyback ride before bed, picking up fresh bakery goods on the way home from church services, or everyone pitching in to do the laundry on Saturday mornings.) These routines offer security because they let family members know when things are normal. Family members feel as though something is missing when one of these routines is not followed. These types of routines give children a sense of comfort and safety, and can help them build positive habits.

Do you remember some of the routines you and your family followed when you were a child? Adapting some of these is a good place to start as you develop some new routines or traditions of your own.

The Importance of Routines and Traditions

Routines and traditions are a way you can give three cheers to your family. The activities you choose don't have to be expensive or complicated. The important thing is that you use routines and traditions to teach your kids how to come together as a family.

Routines and traditions also can be avenues for defining your family's values. Family values are those beliefs and habits family members consider important. They remind family members of what is expected and what their family stands for. They give you and your family direction and help you make good decisions. They also bring to life the idea that everyone in your family is important and loved. This is a powerful message for kids. Family values are the ideals you want to pass on to your children.

We think a good way to help you remember the importance of simple routines and traditions is to tell you the story a parent shared about one of her strongest childhood memories — the summer day decades ago when her mother packed up some peanut butter sandwiches and lemonade and took her two young children into the backyard for an impromptu picnic.

The woman still remembers what it was like to sit on the ground and feel the prickly grass beneath a bedspread, eat her sandwich, and enjoy the cool shade of a big tree on a hot day.

That mother had a knack for making the simple remarkable. We think that's the whole idea around establishing routines and traditions — the ability to create wonderful memories and celebrate without getting lost in the celebration.

Summary

What did you learn from this chapter? If you have a better understanding of what routines and traditions are and how to get them started in your home, then you're off to a great start. If you know that teaching and modeling social skills is a key element in getting your children to follow your family's routines and traditions, then you are one step closer to being able to create fun and memorable times for your children and yourself. If you learned your children should be involved in planning, creating, changing, and maintaining routines and traditions, then you've learned enough to start putting some family routines and traditions into place that are tailor-made for your family.

Make sure you remove any obstacles that could keep you from achieving your goals. These can include unrealistic expectations, a pessimistic attitude, procrastination, and poor planning. And be sure to review other chapters in this book for methods and strategies that can help your family get the most out of the routines and traditions that become part of your family's life.

⌒☞ CHAPTER REVIEW

What is a family routine?

A routine is a custom, habit, schedule, or practice of a family.

How does having a routine help a family?

Routines set expectations, schedules, rules, and specific ways of doing things ahead of time, as part of a daily or weekly routine. Parents spend less time reminding children about what they are supposed to do or not do.

What should parents do to create a family routine?

1. Make sure children have the appropriate social skills to carry out the routine.

2. Use appropriate discipline to address children's positive and negative behavior.

3. Set reasonable expectations.

4. Use charts and contracts to motivate children and monitor their progress.

5. Acknowledge, encourage, and reward cooperation and accomplishments.

6. Use a variety of motivators to encourage children to improve their behavior.

7. Review routines during Family Meetings.

What is a family tradition?

A tradition is a rule, routine, celebration, or habit that makes a family special. Traditions are an important part of family life that help define families and give them unique identities.

Why are routines and traditions important?

Because they help teach kids how they fit into a family, define family values, and demonstrate that when a family comes together, everyone benefits.

 **ACTION PLAN**

1. Take some time to answer the following questions:
   - What is the most important thing you learned in this chapter?
   - What do you plan to do differently as a result of what you've learned?

2. Think about weekday mornings, mealtimes, and bedtimes in your family. Do things usually go pretty smoothly at these times or is there a lot of confusion, whining, nagging, or even fighting going on? If these times are very disorganized in your household, make a list of routines you think might help the situation. Start introducing these routines to your children. You could discuss them at a Family Meeting, ask for your (older)

children's input, and share with your kids what the consequences will be when routines are not followed. Be sure to point out to your children how established routines will directly benefit them.

At your next Family Meeting, schedule a discussion of your family's traditions. Ask your children which traditions are most meaningful or special to them. You could invite the grandparents to your meeting to talk about their childhood memories of special occasions. Or, you could ask for ideas on a new tradition your family would be interested in getting started.

Q&A
FOR PARENTS

Q What should I do if my children completely ignore the routines I'm trying to establish in our home?

A The first thing you should do is assess why this is happening. If your children have the skills necessary to meet the family routine requirements but are merely being defiant, then you should use Corrective Teaching to address the problem behavior. If your children are ignoring a family routine because it conflicts with other important outside activities, or your family's lifestyle doesn't allow your children to accomplish the family routine, then you'll need to adapt and structure the routine to better fit into your family's everyday activities.

Q What should be done when parents disagree on a family routine?

A Before you ever start talking to your children about a family routine, you need to sit down, iron out the details, and come to an agreement. You'll never get your children to follow through on a routine when there is doubt about what needs to be done. When it involves two different households, it's important for both parents to be flexible and to realize there will be two sets of routines. Hopefully, the routines can be made as similar as possible. If parents in different households can't come to a compromise on routines, then it's important to "agree to disagree." This means even though routines will be different, there will still be a commitment to teach routines to the children.

Q Do I really need a routine if things are running smoothly in my home?

A It won't be the end of the world if you don't have a routine, but it never hurts to try and make things better. And we think you'll find that introducing a routine to an already well-run household will provide even more benefits to your family. Also, a routine is important because it helps you clarify some of the teachings, values, traditions, and religious and cultural practices you would like to see your children carry on to their own families someday.

Q One of my children has special needs. How can I make sure he feels he can contribute to the family routine?

A There is always a way to tweak and adjust a routine to make sure everyone in the family is able to contribute in his or her own unique way. Get the child's input about what he thinks he can do to contribute that will make him feel good. Also, ask other family members for their ideas on how to get everyone involved. You'll be pleasantly surprised at some of the creative suggestions and ideas they come up with.

Q My teenagers think following our family's holiday traditions that have been handed down from earlier generations is old-fashioned and corny. How can I convince them these traditions are important to our family and need to be continued?

A Possibly the best way to preserve these traditions and make them more interesting is to first explain to your teens how the traditions started and why they are part of your family's identity. If your teens know more about the people who created the traditions and their reasons for doing so, they might be more inclined to participate and enjoy the traditions. Then, work together as a family to come up with some new (appropriate) traditions, and let your teens lead the way. If they have some ownership of new ways to celebrate and see them becoming part of your family, they may better understand why the older traditions are important.

Chapter 16
Making a Parenting Plan

When a family decides to take a vacation, Mom and Dad and the kids don't just jump in the car, take off down the road, hope they can figure out where they're going, find a place to stay, and find fun things to do when they get there. Before the first bag is packed, the family members sit down to plan the trip and figure out all the details so they'll have few problems and lots of time to enjoy themselves.

Parenting should work the same way. Developing a parenting plan is like having a roadmap you can follow as you assess your own strengths and weaknesses, the strengths and weaknesses of your children, and the best way to teach and care for them. It is a way for you to see how all of your parenting skills can work together to solve parent-child conflicts and to build positive relationships. A plan also enables you to develop a step-by-step positive strategy for preventing and addressing various behavior problems in different situations.

When parents can decide on a consistent approach to things like modeling good behavior and using appropriate discipline, family life can be smoother and parent-child relationships can flourish.

What Is a Parenting Plan?

A parenting plan is an agreement between spouses or among the primary caregivers in a household to use appropriate, effective parenting tools in a consistent manner with children. This means learning and getting good at using the Common Sense Parenting® skills described in this book, and applying the "three C's" of parenting in most situations with children.

The three C's are **courage, commitment,** and **consistency**. In order to get the most out of the parenting skills you are learning in this book, you must have the courage to use them. When relatives and friends question your positive approach, or your children resist and try to "guilt" you out of your newfound confidence, you will need courage to follow through and use what you have learned. Of course, parents should feel confident when committing to a parenting approach that is based on decades of experience, training, and research with children and families from all over the world. But, it is your full commitment to using your parenting skills in everyday life that makes all the difference in your successes at parenting. And once you commit to a positive parenting approach and have the courage to use it (regardless of what anyone else might think), then you'll find you are more consistent in how, when, and what you teach your children.

At first, it's best for parents to write down the main components of their plan so they have something to refer to when they begin using it. The success of any component depends on how well parents apply their skills and tools to it. Components can and should include:

- How to shape problem behaviors so children begin to learn new, more appropriate behaviors.

- How to stay calm in stressful or tense situations.

- How to model the positive behaviors parents want children to learn.

- How to look at children's behavioral problems or parenting problems, determine their cause or root, and figure out the best way to solve them.

- How to accept that everyone in a family has his or her own distinct personality, and that the differences between parents and between parents and their children should not hinder family life.

A parenting plan also lays out clear guidelines that ensure both parents (or other caregivers) are "on the same page" when it comes to giving consequences — both positive and negative — and each parent supports the other's decisions regarding discipline, rules, and tolerances.

While a parenting plan provides a "blueprint" for what to do in specific situations, it also should be flexible enough to meet the changing needs of parents and children. Many factors can play a role in children's behavior and how parents respond. Parents who are too rigid in their parenting style sometimes fail to consider circumstances that might explain why a child is behaving a certain way or why a consequence should be modified to fit a particular situation or behavior. Changes also happen as children get older and more mature. The way parents discipline their kids and praise them for good behavior when they are toddlers and in elementary school will change somewhat when the children reach junior high and high school. Consistency and structure are the keys to good parenting, but flexibility is what allows parents to modify their skills to best fit each situation or problem.

Putting Your Plan Together

The best and easiest way to create a parenting plan is to build it around one child behavior at a time. While parenting plans can be used to address both positive and negative behaviors, most parents develop a plan because they are having trouble dealing with a problem behavior they want to stop or replace with a positive behavior. By tackling one behavior at a time, you can keep your plan simple and focused. If this is the first time you're trying to develop a parenting plan, moving slowly and staying focused on a simple problem behavior will allow you to get a feel for what works well and what does not. Then you can use your early parenting plans as models when you attempt to change your children's more serious problem behaviors.

Identify the Problem

The first step in creating your plan is to identify the problem you want to address. Think of a behavior you would like to change; one your child uses frequently or one that's serious or dangerous. For example, it might be that your son constantly argues and whines when you tell him he can't do or have something. Or, your daughter might be having trouble making friends at school. The first step to a good and effective parenting plan is to put your finger on and describe the problem behavior.

Identify the Alternative Appropriate Behavior

Next, decide what alternative behavior your child needs to learn in order to change the problem behavior. For example, if your child argues and whines when you tell him *"No,"* the alternative behaviors would be to have him look at you, calmly listen, say *"Okay"* without arguing, and, if he really disagrees, talk to you about it later. When you put all of these positive behaviors together, they make up the social skill of "Accepting 'No' for an Answer."

Use Consequences

Next, consider a variety of consequences that might motivate your children to be more cooperative. Keep in mind that consequences should be reasonable in size, important to a child, occur immediately after the behavior, and be contingent on the child's behavior and not your emotions, feelings, or perceptions. Remember, when you have to use a large negative consequence in response to severe or frequent behaviors, make sure you also provide your child with positive correction (a chance to earn back some of the privilege that is taken away) to motivate better behavior.

Prevent Problems

Another step to add to your parenting plan is using Preventive Teaching to help your child avoid problem behaviors in the future. Your child might need to learn more than one behavior or skill in order to address a complex problem like stealing, dishonesty, or bullying. So, it's important that your child practices a new skill several times before he or she uses it in a real-life situation. Also, teach one skill at a time. Kids get overloaded and have a hard time learning when too many skills are thrown their way all at once or in a short period of time. Finally, introduce each new skill during neutral times.

Encourage Good Behavior

Follow up and, over time, replace tangible positive consequences with encouragement and praise. Use Effective Praise to encourage your child's positive improvements, attempts to do better, and things your child already does well. Effective Praise lets your child know what you want him or her to continue doing, which behaviors meet your approval, and your expectations for future behavior. You also can use an occasional reward to reinforce outstanding behavior.

Correct Problem Behavior

Expect your child to have problems from time to time maintaining the positive behaviors or skills you've taught and practiced with him or her. When this happens, stop and address the problem by using Corrective Teaching. Be sure to teach to the problem as soon as you notice it so your child isn't tempted to test your limits, possibly making things worse.

Stay Calm

Children don't always readily accept correction from their parents. In fact, your child might get very angry and things might get worse before they get better. That's the time to move to Teaching Self-Control. This will help both you and your child calm down and eventually be able to return to teaching. This is especially true when you both have a plan to stay calm.

In addition to these specific steps, a parenting plan also can help you:

- Plan for how you will consistently use **Preventive Teaching** to help your child learn appropriate replacement behaviors and social skills. Practice with your child so he or she is comfortable using the skills in various situations.

- Plan for how you will consistently use **Effective Praise** to encourage your child's attempts at and improvements in using targeted positive behaviors.

- Plan for how you will consistently use **Corrective Teaching** to address your child's misbehaviors.

- Plan for the times when your child might lose control of his or her emotions and refuse to use the skills you've taught. This is when you would use the parenting skill of Teaching Self-Control. Make sure you've provided your child with plenty of opportunities to practice how to calm down and that you have a plan for keeping yourself calm during these stressful situations.

Why Is a Parenting Plan Necessary?

Having a parenting plan will give you confidence and provide you with the appropriate support you need to strengthen your parenting style. This doesn't mean you will have an answer to every problem you will ever face. What a good parenting plan gives you is a basic foundation for creating and using teaching tools that best fit your family's needs and routines.

Having a plan also gives you a starting point for your approach to parenting and for measuring your children's progress. You can "tweak" your plan and your approach as your children improve on their behaviors, and as they grow and their needs become more complex. At certain times, you will find you need to use some skills more often than others with a particular child. Or, you may find you can consistently use some skills, even when situations change.

Parenting plans can benefit any family situation. But in two-parent families or families where there are multiple caregivers, having a consistent plan gives parents a way to agree on how to approach various situations with similar basic tools, even though their deliveries may be slightly different. This can cut down on a child's ability to manipulate one parent or the other, which is half the battle.

How Does a Parenting Plan Work?

Here's an example of how a parenting plan might work.

Situation: Your son lies to you on a regular basis.

1. The problem behavior is dishonesty.

2. You will teach your son the skill of "Being Honest" and the behaviors of that skill. The steps might include: 1) accurately tell all the facts; 2) don't omit or add any information; 3) offer the truth without being asked; and 4) be willing to calmly accept responsibility for your behavior.

3. Using Preventive Teaching, you can have your son practice this skill three times each day before he can use privileges like watching television, talking or texting on the phone, using the computer, and/ or playing with friends. You might say something like: *"Tyler, I want you to learn to be honest. This means you should tell all the facts, don't omit or add any information, offer the truth without being asked, and calmly take responsibility for what you've done. When you're honest, people are*

more willing to trust you. Let's practice this skill now. What would you tell me if I asked if you had finished doing your homework?"

4. You will use Effective Praise when your son is being honest, making improvements, and attempting to use the steps of being honest. You may say something like: *"Thanks Tyler! You told the truth without me asking you! When you're honest, I'm more likely to trust you. Because you told me the truth, you've earned extra time watching television tonight after dinner."*

5. Whenever your son is dishonest, you will use Corrective Teaching to teach him the steps of being honest. You may say something like: *"Tyler, you told me you did your homework, but I know from your teacher's note that is not true. For being dishonest, you've lost the privilege of riding your bike tonight. In the future, I want you to tell the whole truth without me asking; then, calmly accept responsibility for your behavior. When you do this, I'll be more likely to believe you in the future. Let's practice being honest right now. I'm going to ask you what time you went to bed last night. Think about it, then tell me."*

6. If your son gets upset and loses control after earning a negative consequence for not being honest, you will use Teaching Self-Control and put your own Staying Calm Plan into effect. You may say something like: *"It looks like you're too upset to deal with this right now. Take a few deep breaths and some time to calm down. I'll check on you*

in a few minutes. (Once your child is calm, check to see if he or she is willing to cooperate. Then do Follow-Up Teaching.) *Next time you're upset, remember to take a few deep breaths and ask for time to cool down. Let's try it now. Show me what you would do and say.* (Child correctly practices how to stay calm.) *Good! You took some breaths and calmly asked me for some time in your room. Since you didn't stay calm earlier, you've lost the privilege of playing video games tonight."*

When to Use a Parenting Plan

You can use a parenting plan with your children to address most situations, both positive and negative. It's useful anytime you want to plan how to:

- Use clear and specific words to describe your child's misbehavior.

- Spend more time encouraging and praising your children for their positive behavior instead of focusing only on their inappropriate behavior.

- Develop a parenting style that is more preventive than reactive.

- Best handle a crisis or complex situation (a death in the family, plans to move your family to another city, etc.).

- Best deal with chronic, stressful situations like a child's tantrums or ongoing teasing between siblings.

- Prevent problems that involve family routines (daily chores, religious practices), peer issues (bullying, peer pressure), special family events (celebrations, holidays, vacation), or privileges (use of the computer, phone).

Parents usually don't have to turn to their plan when they want to prevent, decrease, and/or stop minor behavior problems that can be handled by using redirection (directing children's attention away from their misbehavior to something positive). In life-threatening situations (depression, suicide ideation, drug and alcohol abuse, chronic conduct disorder, etc.), professional intervention rather than a parenting plan is usually required. Start by talking with your child's doctor or a school counselor. Many local community centers, child care agencies, and hospitals have licensed practitioners on staff. Don't be afraid to ask around so you can find the best and most appropriate help for your child. Your child's problem may be serious enough for you to contact a psychologist or psychiatrist. Remember, all of these people are available to help you when a problem becomes too much for you to handle on your own. (If your child poses a threat to himself or herself or is harming others, contact help immediately.) If you need help in a parenting crisis or need referrals to professional services in your area, call the Boys Town National Hotline® anytime at **1-800-448-3000.**

Summary

A parenting plan is an important ingredient for successfully raising happy, healthy children. It helps create a positive family atmosphere, one filled with tolerance, support, and love. When parents know where they are heading, it makes the journey of parenting smoother and less stressful.

☞ CHAPTER REVIEW

What is a parenting plan?

An agreement between spouses or among the primary caregivers in a household to use appropriate, effective parenting tools in a consistent manner with their children.

Why is it important to have a parenting plan?

A good parenting plan gives you a basic foundation for creating and using teaching tools that best fit your family's needs and routines.

What are the steps to creating a plan?

1. Identify the problem.
2. Identify the alternative appropriate behavior.
3. Use consequences.
4. Plan how to prevent problems.
5. Plan how to encourage good behavior.
6. Plan how to correct problem behavior.
7. Plan how to stay calm (when needed).

☆ ACTION PLAN

1. Take some time to answer the following questions:

   • What is the most important thing you learned in this chapter?

   • What do you plan to do differently as a result of what you've learned?

2. Get started right away on writing a parenting plan for one of your child's problem behaviors. Select the behavior and write down what you will do for each of the seven steps. As needed, go back and review the chapters on Effective Praise, consequences, Preventive Teaching, Corrective Teaching, and staying calm. If things don't go as well as you hoped as you implement your plan, make adjustments as needed. Remember, behavior doesn't change overnight, so be sure you give your plan time to work. Appreciate improvements in behavior even if the problem doesn't disappear completely.

Q&A
FOR PARENTS

Q As a parent, I often feel overwhelmed. Can a parenting plan help me with our family routine?

A Yes. A parenting plan can provide you with a step-by-step way to set up, maintain, and follow up on a family routine, while giving you the flexibility to make changes along the way.

Q My parents didn't use a parenting plan. Why do I need one?

A A parenting plan is helpful when it comes to providing parents and children with a consistent approach to discipline. Today, families are busier than ever, and it's hard to keep everything in a household straight. A parenting plan is an organizational tool for you and your family that can help make your lives less complicated.

Q What if one parent or caregiver doesn't want to use a parenting plan? Should you just give it up or try to use it anyway?

A Giving up is never an answer when developing a good parenting approach — unless it means giving up a bad parenting habit or strategy. Go ahead and press on by using the plan yourself. Hopefully, the other parent will come around when he or she sees how well the kids respond to you. At the very least, you'll feel good about the way you've chosen to discipline your children.

Q What if we try a parenting plan and our child's behavior still doesn't improve?

A Give it time and have patience. It takes time for a child to develop problem behaviors, and it takes time to change them and learn positive alternative behaviors. With some problems, you may need professional help. Don't be afraid to call a school counselor, pastor, therapist, psychologist, or doctor who can guide you in making the best decisions for your children and family.

Q I'm a single parent. Should I discuss my plan with my children?

A That's up to you. It might be best to share your plan with your children once you've come up with some of the basic points. Let your children know that things will change and why they are changing. Sharing how the plan works might help your kids accept the change in your parenting approach with less resistance.

SECTION V

Special Topics

A major part of parenting involves preparing children for what they're going to face outside the friendly confines of family and home. Too often, children fail because they haven't been taught what to do in stressful or potentially dangerous situations "out there." As a parent, you can't always be around when your child must make a decision, solve a problem, or use a particular skill.

Two of the many situations where children must know how to act on their own to be successful and avoid trouble are in school and when dealing with peer pressure. Children tell us they are glad when their parents provide guidance in dealing with real-life problems. That's why you must know what's going on in your child's world, provide support and advice, and be willing to help solve problems he or she encounters. But even that is not enough. You also must be understanding, rather than judgmental and indifferent. Children have to know their parents are on their side, and they truly care about preparing and helping them to make good choices.

How well you help your children succeed in school, handle peer pressure, and deal with other problems they will face depends largely on your ability to use all the parenting skills we've discussed so far in this book. You will use many of the same skills when addressing these areas. But regardless of the situation, the parenting responses we recommend all fall under the **TIME** acronym we discussed in Chapter 1. **TIME stands for Talking, Instructing, Monitoring, and Encouraging.** As a parent, you always must provide clear expectations and positive discipline to help your children learn how to control their impulses and emotions, weigh their options, and consider the possible outcomes of their actions.

Before we discuss the specific areas of school success and peer pressure, here are 10 effective parenting tools every parent can and should use to support their children and enhance their ability to make good decisions on their own. (Most of these tools will be mentioned throughout the next two chapters.)

1. **Tell** your child what you expect from him or her in specific situations, as well as what support you will provide.

2. **Talk** with — not at — your child about what he or she will experience or has experienced without being judgmental or overly emotional.

3. **Listen** to your children's ideas and concerns, regardless of whether you feel they are right or wrong. Listening doesn't mean you agree, but it does show you are concerned and willing to hear what your son or daughter is thinking and feeling.

4. **Model** the positive behaviors you want your child to use. It would be unrealistic to say to your child, "Do as I say, not as I do." Parents must set a good example in order to show their children how expectations can be met in everyday life.

5. **Ask** for help from professionals when you need it. Parents often are too afraid, ashamed, or overwhelmed by their children's behavior to ask for help. Parents aren't expected to have all the answers, but they are expected to help their child look for them.

6. **Motivate** your child to develop a strong foundation for life by teaching him or her character-building skills. When children can govern themselves based on their own personal values and the content of their character, they will be less susceptible to pressure from others.

7. **Be on hand** to offer assistance, guidance, and encouragement. Parents who know their children and are available to them are better at parenting in both routine and difficult situations.

8. **Allow** your child to accept responsibility for his or her behavior. Don't make excuses or try to undo what your child has done wrong, but be there to guide him or her in the right direction without taking over.

9. **Remind** your child to think before acting. Occasionally use a "mini-reminder" to prompt what you've taught your child to do before he or she encounters problems. Don't nag, but when it

is appropriate, let your child know you are aware of his or her struggles and are around to help.

10. **Follow up** on your child's progress or concerns. Parents must stay involved in their children's daily lives in order to know how to help them. Whenever possible, provide clear written and verbal instructions about the rules you set, the consequences for breaking them, and the rewards for keeping them.

Teens and Healthy Relationships

Healthy relationships are those that involve mutual care and consideration. They make participants happy. They build up confidence and feelings of self-worth. They do not make one person in the relationship feel used, taken for granted, or insecure.

Physical or emotional abuse has no place in a relationship. If someone hits or verbally assaults his or her friend once, chances are it will continue to happen. Your child deserves better than this and should get out of damaging or dangerous relationships that involve physical or emotional abuse.

To protect and prepare your child, share the following tips on how to develop a positive relationship and help it grow in a healthy way:

- **Take time** — Get to know the other person slowly. Don't rush or allow the other person to rush you.

- **Be sure the relationship involves give and take** — Create a healthy balance in interests, likes, and expectations between you and the other person.

- **Don't spend a lot of time worrying about the relationship** — It is just one part of your life; you have other responsibilities as well.

- **Realize relationships constantly change** — People change. Relationships need to adjust to these changes.

- **Look at past relationships that were positive** — Model new relationships after past positive relationships. Consider relationships that did not work and identify why they did not work to avoid repeating the same mistakes.

- **Write down why certain people make good friends** — Seek the same qualities in new relationships.

- **Write down things people do that are not acceptable** — Avoid people who possess these qualities.

Happy, healthy relationships take work. The persons involved must understand there is give and take, and they may have to compromise sometimes. People in healthy relationships want what is best for their friends. They want their friends to be happy. A genuine friend will like their friends for who they already are; they don't expect or require their friends to change to please them.

Everyone deserves to be safe and happy. Identify positive, healthy qualities in friendships and teach them to your kids. Also, model these qualities in your own relationships so your children understand what they look like and why they are important.

We have created a relationship questionnaire to help your children understand how people in their lives interact with them. Please read or copy this and talk to your child about their relationships. If you suspect he or she is in an abusive relationship, call or have your child call a domestic violence hotline or the toll-free Boys Town National Hotline® at **1-800-448-3000** for help. As always, if you or someone you love is in immediate danger, always call 911 for help.

Youth Relationship Questionnaire

The following questions are meant to help you understand when a relationship is unhealthy. If you answer "Yes" to some of the questions below, you may be in a relationship that is bad for you.

1. Do I ever feel used or treated like an object?

2. Am I spending too much time thinking about the way I'm treated in this relationship?

3. Have I lost interest in things I used to like? Do I feel isolated from my old friends?

4. Do I ever feel like I'm being intimidated or forced into doing something I don't want to do?

5. Am I embarrassed about things my friend does to me or with me? Does my friend make fun of me and put me down in front of others?

6. Have I ever felt unsafe or been afraid of what my friend might do to me?

7. Have I ever been threatened with words or physical force?

8. Has my friend ever forced or tried to force me into doing something sexual by threatening to end the relationship?

9. Does my friend ever get extremely mad at things, and I don't understand why? Does he or she take it out on me or others?

10. Does my friend make excuses for what he or she has done? Does my friend fail to realize when he or she has hurt me? Do I get blamed for what happened?

11. Does my friend blame his or her violent behavior on alcohol or drugs?

12. Has my friend ever hit, slapped, pushed, or choked me?

Learn more about this topic in *Dating! 10 Helpful Tips for a Successful Relationship,* by Laura J. Buddenberg and Alesia K. Montgomery, and *There Are No Simple Rules for Dating My Daughter!,* by Laura J. Buddenberg and Kathleen M. McGee. Both books are available through the Boys Town Press® (boystownpress.org).

Chapter 17

Helping Children Succeed in School

"I hate school! I'm never going back!"
"I just can't get this stuff. It's too hard!"
"Nobody likes me. I'm always getting picked on."

Does your child have difficulty getting homework done, obeying teachers, following rules, or getting along with classmates? Any of these school-related troubles can spill over and create plenty of problems at home.

For some children, problems at school are directly tied to academic deficits. These children might have difficulty reading or comprehending what they've read, recalling information for tests, or writing papers. They might need strategic academic assessment and intervention. In these situations, parents always should discuss their concerns with the school counselor, psychologist, principal, and the child's teacher. This "team" can then devise a plan to help the child improve in the areas where he or she is struggling.

Often, however, the problems children experience at school have little to do with their academic ability; they may instead be related to a child's behavior and his or her inability to successfully use certain social skills. For example, many children who perform poorly in the classroom often don't know how to use the basic social skill of "Following Instructions." Simply put, they can't or don't follow instructions to complete homework, prepare and study for tests, regularly attend class, and perform other tasks crucial to academic success. These children also might be disruptive when asking for help or accepting criticism from a teacher, or be off task or daydreaming in class when they should be listening to information that will help them do well.

By and large, some of the most successful students are those who follow instructions and behave well in the classroom. They have learned from their parents, teachers, and other adults what kind of behavior is expected in school and have mastered the basic social skills needed for success there. Children who can use positive social skills have a much better chance of succeeding in the classroom.

Another reason children encounter problems at school is lack of involvement by parents. When parents don't take an active role in their child's educational experience, they send the message that school isn't important. If parents don't see school as an important and essential cog in their child's growth and development, how can they expect their child to see it that way?

What Parents Can Do

There are several things parents can do at home and with the school to help improve their children's academic performance and school behavior, and deal with problems at school as they arise. The remainder of this chapter will discuss a few areas we have identified as crucial in preparing children to meet behavioral and academic expectations in the classroom. We'll also provide some helpful tips on how you can enhance your involvement in your child's education, stay informed about day-to-day school progress, and work with your child's teachers and school to resolve problems.

Get in the Game

It is crucial for you to be "plugged in" to your child's school life. Studies show parental involvement in school is closely tied to children's success in school. Asking your children about their school day is a good place to start, but don't stop there. Visit your child's school. If your child is younger, eat lunch with him or her. Volunteer to help with field trips or other activities where parental supervision is needed (trips to the zoo, weekend dances, science fairs). Join the PTA or some other school-sponsored organization. Make it a point to talk with the school principal and your child's teachers so they know who you are and feel comfortable contacting you should a problem arise. Being involved in your children's education doesn't make you a pest. It means being a source of support for your child, the school, and your child's teachers and administrators.

Target Homework

Studies have shown, and common sense supports, that studying at home can help improve children's performance in school. Here are some tips for helping children get their homework completed regularly and correctly:

- **Establish a central location for completing homework.** Make sure your child has a clean

317

working surface (a kitchen table or a desk in your child's room) and all the supplies he or she needs (a dictionary, calculator, paper, pencils, notebooks, etc.).

- **Keep the area as quiet as possible for study time.** If necessary, shut off the TV and radio in other rooms and try to limit other distractions, such as the telephone. Keep other children occupied by reading them a story (if they're younger) or having them play outside.

- **Set aside a specific amount of time for studying and homework each school night** (typically, Sunday through Thursday nights). For elementary school children, study time might last 30 to 45 minutes; for junior high students, 45 to 75 minutes; and for high school students, 60 to 90 minutes or more. Increase the amount of time if your child needs longer to complete assignments.

- **Make sure your child starts study time on time,** but be flexible. When things come up that prevent your child from studying at the designated time, adjust your schedule. The main point is for your child to understand that homework is his or her responsibility and it has to be done.

- **Divide study time into smaller periods for children who have difficulty concentrating for long periods of time.** For example, some children, especially younger ones, may do better studying for 15 minutes, taking a short break, then studying for another 15 minutes. If they know they'll get a break, they may be more likely to concentrate during the actual study time.

- **Schedule study time to fit your family's routines.** Doing homework right after school works best for some children. But if a child is involved in after-school activities, or both parents work outside the home and they want to be there to help, an early evening study time might work better. Picking a time when there are few interruptions and when children are most likely to concentrate increases the probability homework will get completed.

- **Remember "Grandma's Rule"** ("If you finish your homework, then you can play video games") when setting up study time. Children are more likely to do homework if you schedule study time before they can watch TV, play on the computer, talk or text on the phone, or go to a friend's house.

- **Be available and watch for opportunities to praise** your child for staying on task and doing a good job. This shows your child you truly care about schoolwork and you notice and appreciate his or her efforts.

- **Set a positive example.** Read a book, write a letter, balance the checkbook, work on the computer, or make a grocery list while your child is doing homework. Leave the TV and radio off.

- **Provide help if your child is having trouble.** If a question you can't answer comes up, have your child call a classmate or the teacher. Then, have your child explain the answer to you so you both understand what he or she is doing.

- **Always set aside time for learning and reading.** If children do not bring assignments home, or if they tell you they've completed all their homework in school, have them do projects for extra credit, or read books, magazines, or newspapers. The goal is to make learning an ongoing activity. If the first step toward establishing a life-long habit of reading for a child comes from reading a sports magazine, then start there. In time, he or she may be willing to branch out to other kinds of magazines and books.

Here are some other activities for children who say they have no homework:

- Reading aloud to a younger brother or sister.
- Reading a newspaper article about world events, nutrition, youth problems, or any other interesting topic.
- Writing letters to grandparents, friends, or relatives.
- Cutting coupons and adding up the amount of money saved.
- Helping a brother or sister with homework or tutoring a friend or neighbor.
- Writing in a journal or diary.
- Making a list of the things to do for the week.

- Doing something fun and educational with Mom or Dad.

Explain and Enforce Rules

When children misbehave at school, it's either because they don't understand the rules and expectations for school behavior or they choose not to follow them. Either way, it is up to you as a parent to discuss with your child why appropriate behavior is important at school and to teach and practice the skills that make such behavior possible.

The place to start your child's education of these issues is with a review of the school's code of conduct. This should specifically spell out what is allowed and what is not allowed on school grounds and at school activities. It also should list violations and the consequences that go with them. Remember to explain these rules in language that fits your child's age and developmental level. Making sure your child is aware of the rules that make up the code of conduct, and reviewing them with him or her from time to time, can head off many problems and make life at school smoother.

In addition to the code of conduct, each teacher will have his or her own rules for the classroom. Good behavior is necessary for all students so teachers can create a positive learning environment and keep disruptions to a minimum. The less time teachers spend correcting students, the more time they can spend teaching. All students benefit when everyone obeys and cooperates with classroom rules and shows respect to the teacher and each other.

That brings us to the skills and behaviors children should be learning in order to succeed in the classroom and how they should be taught. These skills and behaviors are the same ones you expect your child to use at home and out in public. As we said earlier, problems in school most often are the result of children not knowing which skills to use or how to use them. So, before your child — whether he or she is a kindergartner or a junior in high school — heads off on that first day of classes, a lot of teaching should take place. This is an ideal situation for Preventive Teaching and practice. While there are a number of skills that can benefit children, we would suggest focusing on five basic skills: Following Instructions, Getting Along with Others, Accepting Criticism, Showing Respect, and Asking Permission.

Most importantly, make sure you praise your child for good school behavior. In the past, you may have focused only on misbehavior and what your child did wrong at school and sometimes ignored what your child did well. Praise reinforces good behavior and makes it more likely your child will repeat it. It also lets your child know that you notice when he or she improves or does something well and helps make school a positive experience.

Partner with Teachers

A child's teacher is a parent's biggest ally when it comes to helping children succeed in school. That's why it is so important to start off a parent-teacher relationship on a positive note.

Attending the open house that almost every school offers at the beginning of the school year will probably be your first opportunity to meet your child's teacher (or teachers). Introduce yourself and be sure to mention the teacher may call you whenever necessary. Give the teacher an index card with the telephone number(s) and/or email address where you can be reached. Explain that you want to stay informed about your child's progress, and ask if you may call the teacher during his or her free period. If acceptable, call or email the teacher and ask how your child is doing at the end of the first week of school.

During the school year, you'll have many other opportunities to talk with your child's teacher. Probably the most important of these is the parent-teacher conference. This is a time when you can have a one-on-one conversation with not only your child's teacher(s) but also with coaches, the school counselor, or even the principal, about your child's behavior and academic progress. Discuss specific things your child is doing well or needs to improve. This is your opportunity to ask questions, work on problems, and let your child and the teacher know you are actively involved in the educational process. Attending these conferences is the best way to stay informed about what's happening with your child in school, and demonstrates to your child and the school staff you believe school is important.

School picnics, holiday concerts, school plays, sports activities, science fairs, and fund-raising events are just a few of the more informal times when you can touch base with teachers and other school staff members to reinforce your commitment to helping your child find success.

You also can periodically share with the teacher what you are teaching your child at home. If you are teaching your child skills like "Following Instructions" and "Asking for Help," discuss with the teacher how he or she might reinforce them at school. During the school year, let the teacher know when major events occur in your child's life, such as the death of a relative or other emotional situations. Always thank teachers for the work they do and the time they spend with your child.

Unfortunately, the first time some parents talk to a teacher is when the teacher or school contacts them about a problem involving their child. Being proactive and making the first move to develop a positive relationship with a teacher lets him or her know that you're concerned about your child's education. If your child does have problems in school, it may be easier to resolve them if you and the teacher know each other and can work together. And when a teacher calls with good news, make sure you let your child know how important that is.

Address Problems

There may be a time when you receive an unexpected call from school asking you to meet with a teacher or an administrator to discuss a problem. These types of meetings can make parents nervous, angry, confused, and apprehensive. Here is a list of helpful hints to prepare you for such events and make them more positive:

- **Take time to get calm.** You are much more likely to help solve a problem if you can remain calm and focus on a solution during any meeting with teachers and administrators.

- **Find out the exact nature of the problem.** Be sure you talk with the teacher or school administrator who is involved with the situation. If he or she is unable to explain the situation clearly, ask specific questions to help you understand the problem. The focus here is not to challenge whether the problem occurred, but to understand what the problem is.

- **Ask the teachers or administrators for suggestions for solving the problem or improving the situation that can be done at school and at home.** Some teachers and administrators have had a great deal of experience with certain problems. They work with a variety of children and may have effective ways for how both you and school staff can constructively respond to your child's particular problem.

- **Offer your suggestions for solving the problem or improving the situation.** Trust your instincts; no one knows your child as well as you. Your past experiences with your child, both successful and unsuccessful, will contribute to coming up with an effective strategy for solving the problem. Be open to new ideas from the school staff, but also share your opinion about the proposed solution.

- **Thank the school staff for their time and concern.** Calling a parent to the school is typically stressful for everyone involved. Let the staff know you appreciate their efforts on behalf of your child.

- **Don't take sides or defend your child's behavior.** Remember, the goal of the meeting with your child's teacher or school administrator is to get information, solve the immediate problem, and look for ways to help your child do better in the future. This is not the time to side with the school and complain about your child, or take your child's side and attack his or her teachers or the school. Work together with the school staff to find an effective solution. Then try your best, and ask your child to try his or her best, to follow through with the agreed-upon plan.

- **After the meeting, talk with your child about the problem and the proposed solution.** Keep in touch with the school staff and ask them to do the same with you. Your goal at this point is to help the child learn from the experience and to prevent the problem from happening again.

Whatever the situation or reason, calling or meeting with a teacher or a school administrator sends a clear message to everyone — your children and school staff — that you are interested and involved in your children's education.

Using School Notes

Communication is the key to a positive relationship between parents and schools. School notes are a great way to keep the lines of communication open and to keep track of your child's progress and problems. (Studies have shown school notes accompanied by possible positive and negative consequences have a positive effect on children's school behavior and academic performance.)

School notes can be formal or informal. A formal school note can include a list of the child's classes and space where the teacher can comment on how the child is doing in class or with homework. The teacher fills out the note and sends it home with the student. Parents can then acknowledge the teacher's comments and write their own comments on the note, which the child returns to the teacher. Notes can be completed daily, weekly, or monthly, whatever schedule fits the needs of your child and the teacher. Talk to teachers ahead of time to explain why you are using a school note and to work out a schedule.

It helps to keep school note information brief and specific. Typically, teachers don't have the time to fill out lengthy explanations of your child's behavior. Make it easy for the teacher to quickly circle positive or negative behaviors listed on the note. Have the teacher initial the note or circled items. Also, ask the teacher to call you if he or she needs to give you more detailed information.

Parents who want information about their child's classes, but don't want their child to carry a note every day, can use an informal school note. These usually are written or emailed requests for information from the parent to the teacher. Teachers also can use them to request information from parents. In either case, the adults are sharing information about schoolwork or behavior. Often, just letting your children know you are monitoring their schoolwork can have a positive influence.

When using a school note, it is important to make your child's privileges contingent on taking the note to school and bringing it home, attending classes, behaving well, and completing homework.

Here are two examples of school notes. The first is for younger children or children who have only one teacher each day. The second is for older children or children who have several teachers during the school day. Adapt either one to meet your needs.

School Note

Dear Mrs. Miller,

We're trying to help Michael do better in school. Please circle "yes" for each behavior Michael regularly uses each day and "no" for behaviors he does not regularly use. Then initial and send this note home with Michael each day. Thanks.

— Sally Johnson

	Stays in seat	Follows instructions	Turns in homework	Teacher's initials
MONDAY	yes/no	yes/no	yes/no	
TUESDAY	yes/no	yes/no	yes/no	
WEDNESDAY	yes/no	yes/no	yes/no	
THURSDAY	yes/no	yes/no	yes/no	
FRIDAY	yes/no	yes/no	yes/no	

The following note not only allows teachers to let parents know how their child is doing at school, but also lets parents inform the teachers about the child's homework habits and areas of difficulty.

School Note

Teachers,

We are trying to help Michael do better in all of his classes. Please note whether Michael did these things in your class during this past week and then initial the last column. Please call us at 555-1212 if you have any questions. Thanks.

— Sally Johnson

		Got to class on time	Completed homework	Followed instructions	Teacher's initials
	1				
	2				
PERIOD	3				
	4				
	5				
	6				
	7				

Study Report: Here are the days and times Michael spent doing his homework or studying at home this week.

SUN.	MON.	TUES.	WED.	THURS.
_____	_____	_____	_____	_____

My child is working on:

Helping Children Through School Transitions

School presents a continuing series of changes and challenges for children. They move from preschool to elementary to junior high to high school, and then on to college, a job, or vocational school. Each year, children must make the transition from summer play to structured school rooms. Every school day, they go from one subject or classroom to another. For some children, these changes can lead to behavior problems or can interfere with their learning. Here are some tips for helping children through these transitions:

- **Be positive about school.** Talk with your children about the good things that happen at school. Tell them about some of your positive experiences in school.

- **Start talking about school as early in your child's life as possible.** Set the expectation that your child will get a good education. Always make the prospect of going to school (or going back to school) exciting and fun.

- **Expect your child to experience some stress that is related to school, tests, friends, and homework.** Be understanding when they tell you about their frustrations. If your child suffers severe or chronic school-related stress, you should get professional help for him or her.

- **Listen to your children and what they tell you about school**. Sometimes, it just helps to let them talk about what's going on in their lives. Be supportive and attentive. Try not to be judgmental or get upset at whatever they might say.

- **Visit your children's school.** Find out about the school day, the administration, and naturally, your children's teachers. Keep the lines of communication open (school activities, school notes, telephone calls, and meetings).

- **Praise the good things your children do.** Especially focus on their attempts to improve their behavior and successfully solve their problems. Family Meetings are a good place to acknowledge these positive steps.

Summary

Children will spend a major portion of their waking hours in school as they grow up. Your involvement and attention to your children's schoolwork and positive behavior, and your commitment to working with school staff, are keys to helping them succeed there.

The suggestions in this chapter are based on research studies and our experiences at Boys Town's sites where we provide a home and schooling for more than a thousand children each year. These are general guidelines and do not cover every type of school problem that can occur. Consider them a starting point for improving your child's school performance and behavior, and your relationship with your child's school. If you are experiencing more serious school problems with your child and the suggestions in this chapter don't seem to be improving the situation, be sure to talk with a school counselor or another professional who can help with your child's particular problems.

☞ CHAPTER REVIEW

What is one of the major reasons children struggle in school?

They cannot correctly use basic social skills like "Following Instructions," "Accepting Criticism," and "Asking for Help."

What is one way you can help your child succeed in school?

Being actively and positively involved in your child's school experience.

What are three things you can do to help your child improve his or her homework skills?

1) Be available to help your child; 2) Set a positive example by reading, writing a letter, or balancing the checkbook; and 3) Show your children how to organize and prioritize their homework time and materials.

☆ ACTION PLAN

1. Take some time to answer the following questions:
   - What is the most important thing you learned in this chapter?
   - What do you plan to do differently as a result of what you've learned?

2. Each day this week, spend 5-10 minutes reviewing the school day with your child. Start the conversation by

asking the child to tell you three fun or interesting things he or she did or learned during the day. Then ask if your child encountered any difficulties — these could involve concepts or assignments presented in class, disagreements with classmates, discipline from the teacher, etc. Make brief notes to yourself at the end of these conversations. Also observe how much time and effort your child puts into his or her homework and what questions, if any, the child asks. Check over each night's homework.

At the end of the week, review your notes and observations. If you see recurring problems, decide if you need to meet or talk with one or more of your child's teachers or set up a school note system. If so, follow through with your decision.

Q&A
FOR PARENTS

Q **I'm a single parent who works. How can I get involved at my child's school if I'm working all day?**

A Even without the help of a spouse, there are ways to get involved that fit into your schedule. Ask your child's teacher or the school principal about evening or weekend activities or functions where you can help out. These might include PTA and school board meetings, school projects (removing graffiti, cleaning up a playground), book drives, fundraising, chaperoning, and many others. Choosing to participate in just one such activity will provide you with an opportunity to meet school staff members.

Q **My son is struggling in school and I'm not sure if it's because of his behavior or because he's not capable of doing the work. What should I do?**

A The best way to start is to contact your son's teacher and discuss the problem. Ask the teacher to identify your son's strengths and the areas where he needs to improve. From there, you and the teacher can work on a plan for helping your son do better in school. For example, you and the teacher might agree to use a school note to monitor your child's progress and setbacks, or you could make changes in his homework routine. You also can use positive consequences to reward good school reports and negative consequences to correct and change negative reports. The key is to communicate and work with the school to help your child succeed.

Q How can I get my daughter to tell me what's going on at school? She says everything is fine and I know it isn't.

A Set aside some one-on-one time during the evening to discuss your daughter's school day. Make sure it's a time when she's willing to talk. Don't force the conversation; let it happen naturally. Ask open-ended questions; for example, "What was your favorite class today?" or "Tell me what you studied in math today." These kinds of questions will obtain more information than if you ask general questions like, "How was school?" or "What did you do today?" Also, ask questions about certain parts of school you know your child enjoys. This can open the door to talking about other school topics. For example, ask her for an update on classmates, friends, or extracurricular activities. Then ask her which teachers or classes she likes best or dislikes most.

Q My child struggles with homework. What can I do to help him?

A Organize and tailor your child's study time to fit his learning ability, temperament, and age. Some children can study for hours while other children need frequent breaks in order to retain what they've learned and be able to stay on task. Make sure your son understands his homework instructions and check all his work before allowing him to move on to entertaining activities like watching television or playing video games. Also, create a positive environment for studying. Remove distractions and noisy activities during study time. Study time should occur at the same time each evening. Have him study in a designated area that's well lit and comfortable. Make sure he has all the materials he needs to complete his homework. Finally, use lots of Effective Praise (and rewards like a special snack, later bedtime, more computer time) when he puts in the time and successfully completes his homework.

CHAPTER 18

Handling Peer Pressure

M ost parents see peer pressure as purely negative. To those parents, it involves someone telling, persuading, or verbally forcing their child to do or consider doing something wrong or inappropriate. But peer pressure has another side. Just as easily as it can influence children to be "bad," it also can persuade them to avoid trouble and not follow the crowd. Friends can encourage one another to do good things, to try harder in extracurricular activities or schoolwork, and to avoid other youth who might not have their best interests at heart. This kind of peer pressure is very healthy.

What's difficult for most children is knowing when peer pressure is a good thing and when it's time to resist and walk away. They don't always have the necessary tools and experience to know when to say "Yes" and when to say "No." That's where parents can make a huge difference. Parents who have a loving, trusting relationship with their children can ask the tough questions and penetrate the very barrier that children try to put up to keep parents out. This doesn't mean you are always going to know everything about what your child is up to, but it does give you a starting place for finding out.

Parents can't make negative peer pressure go away; it is a natural part of growing up. But you can help your child learn how to deal with it. Later in this chapter, we'll discuss some strategies for doing that. First, we'll describe "traditional" peer pressure and some new kinds of negative peer pressure born from the technology age. We'll also look at how peer pressure can reach into your child's life even when no one is physically around.

Personal and Cultural Peer Pressure

Everyone knows what personal peer pressure is. A group of young children are standing around and a couple of them get the idea to go tip over Mrs. Smith's flower pots. The chief plotters try to convince the others they can't possibly get caught and really, tipping over a couple of flower pots is just a harmless prank. Pretty soon, most the group has agreed, and they all go to work on the one or two holdouts whose consciences are telling them this might not be a good idea. Then comes the inevitable hard sell: ***"What, are you chicken? Are you afraid old lady Smith is going to chase you down? C'mon, what's the big deal? Are you a baby or something?"*** After a few minutes, one of two things happens: The holdouts give in and the scheme goes forward, or they tell the others the plan is stupid and they go home.

Although Mrs. Smith (and the parents of the children who get caught) might not think so, this is a pretty harmless scenario. The bigger problem with peer pressure is when the same group (or even just a couple of children) gets together and someone decides they should get some beer or some drugs, cheat on a test at school, damage property, steal, hurt someone, or dare someone to have sex. In these instances, giving in to peer pressure can have some major consequences. This is the stuff that makes parents cringe and lie awake at night wondering if their child will do the right thing.

Negative "personal" peer pressure has been and always will be around. It involves face-to-face contact and communication between two or more people, where a person or a group of persons is trying to convince, persuade, cajole, tease, bully, or shame a person or group of persons into doing something that is against the rules, illegal, or morally or ethically wrong.

But what about the persuasive messages that bombard your child on the Internet, in TV ads and programs, in popular music and music videos, in magazines, and in marketing and advertising specifically aimed at young people? Oftentimes, the common theme is: "Everyone your age (peers) has a certain product or is doing something that makes them cool; if you don't buy it or do it, you're a loser." If these messages are predominantly negative and potentially harmful, and they constantly make your child feel like he or she has to act or look a certain way to fit in or be cool, then parents have another problem.

Television, the Internet, and social media have made communication instant and global. This technology has ushered in a whole new kind of impersonal, cultural peer pressure. The voices of the masses and the mass media now can be constantly channeled into your home and into your child's head. This kind of peer pressure tries to tell your child what to wear, what to eat, what to watch on TV or in a movie theater, what to drink, what to think, how to act, who to date, how to treat the opposite sex, and how to regard parents. It can sometimes be more powerful than personal peer pressure, and it is relentless because there are few places a child can go where it isn't present.

So now parents are faced with a double-barreled problem when it comes to negative peer pressure. What can you do to maintain your influence in your child's life and educate him or her about how best to handle the negative personal and cultural peer pressure messages that are all around?

Parenting vs. Peer Pressure

As with most parenting problems, the best advice we can give you is to follow the parenting approach and strategies described in this book. Building a strong relationship with your child, teaching and practicing social skills, and praising positive behaviors and correcting negative behaviors consistently and with effective consequences form a solid foundation for handling any parenting problem.

But in the area of peer pressure, there are some specific ways you can prepare your child to make good decisions and to know when peer pressure means bad news. There is also much you can do to maintain your influence in your child's life and to build a trust that lets him or her know you are always there to help when decisions are hard to make. Here are some suggestions for helping your children handle negative peer pressure. Remember to make sure any strategy you use fits your child's age and developmental level.

Spend Time Together

Studies indicate children who feel close to their parents are less likely to be negatively influenced by other children than children who don't have good relationships with their parents. Children who have strong relationships with their parents also are more likely to be confident in their abilities and able to solve problems on their own. Strong, trusting, and respectful parent-child relationships don't just happen overnight. They are the result of all the teaching you do with your children and all the time you spend with them. Parents have a powerful influence on their children and this greatly affects the types of decisions kids make.

Many children live in a household where both parents work. Many others live in single-parent households. Parents have many demands on their time. Regardless of how much time we'd like to spend with our children, life's obligations and obstacles sometimes trip us up. The only way to ensure you will have time with your children is to make time. Make it a priority. It's not something you can put off until tomorrow. Any parent with grown children can tell you how fast time flies, and before you know it, your children will be on their own, too.

As children get older, they become more involved with outside activities and friends. They can slip farther and farther away from their parents' guidance and influence. This is part of the normal progression from childhood to adulthood, as children become independent by learning who they are and what they believe in. How well children respond to the rest of the world as they grow up depends a great deal on the quality of their relationships with their parents. If you are the parent of an older child who always seems to be busy and is never around you, find something you both enjoy and do it together. Go fishing, shopping, out to a movie, for a walk, out to eat; it doesn't matter what you do as long as you are spending time together.

You can also schedule "micro-dates." These are 15- or 20-minute blocks of time for you and your children to talk or just be together. Micro-dates give parents and children small amounts of time with each other that fit into a busy schedule. For example, when you pick up your daughter after school, take the long way home, stop and get a soda and snack, and talk about each other's day. With a younger child, you can read a book or set a timer and play a five-minute game of hide-and-seek with him or her. The more time you spend with your children, the more likely they are to open up about what's happening in their lives, and the more guidance you can provide for battling negative peer pressure.

Use Preventive Teaching and SODAS

Some of the time you spend with your children should be used to discuss problems and concerns they might face. This gives you an opportunity to offer advice and reinforce your family's morals and values, the core of what you believe in. Your children's standards of acceptable behavior emerge and are solidified from what you teach and what you say and do.

Because you know your children's good and bad qualities, their tendencies, and their likes and dislikes, you can use Preventive Teaching to prepare them for times when they have to make difficult choices. Teach them how to say "No" and mean it. Teach them how to appropriately disagree, share their opinions, and help friends who are in need. These can be powerful skills when your children can use them confidently and consistently. They can help your children not only avoid and resist negative influences, both personal and cultural, but also convince others to do the same.

You also can prepare your children by teaching them how to come up with "one-liners" they can use in given situations. For example, if your teenage daughter is being pressured by her boyfriend to skip school, she can say,

"If you really care about me, you would want me to keep my grades up," or *"You are behind in science class already and I don't want you to get further behind."* If all else fails, you can tell your child it's okay to use you as the ultimate reason for not wanting to give in to pressure. Your daughter could tell her boyfriend, *"My parents will ground me for a month,"* or *"My parents would freak and I wouldn't be able to spend time with you on the weekend."* The important thing is to let your children know they have lots of ways to say "No" if they take the time to think ahead.

Children should have a variety of options and solutions for the problems they face with peer pressure. There is no perfect solution that can be used in every situation. That's why it is crucial for children to have a problem-solving strategy like **SODAS** (see Chapter 13). **SODAS** provides the structure children need to organize their thoughts and make a rational decision, rather than just doing the first thing that comes to mind. With **SODAS**, children can identify the situation, come up with options, assess the advantages and disadvantages of each option, and decide on a solution. Reinforce your child's use of **SODAS** and practice this skill with him or her often.

Even when children are confident and have a plan for making decisions, they still might face tough situations. Just because parents and their children practice how to say "No," it doesn't mean their friends will accept it right away. They might nag and badger or be coy and convincing until your child feels like giving in. So, you have to teach your child to stay calm and confident, and to be just as persistent with his or her answers. This also might be a good time to talk with your child about whether others who don't respect his or her decisions are true friends.

As your children get older, they will find dangers lurking around every corner. Don't let them be caught unaware. The evils of drugs, drinking, gangs, sex, violence, cheating, and other illegal or immoral activities permeate today's culture. And there are a lot of other less serious areas that can mean trouble. Your children will feel the pressure from their peers to get involved. They want to be liked so the temptation to go along with the crowd is always there. Give them the benefit of your experience and knowledge by using Preventive Teaching and **SODAS** to teach them the difference between good friends and harmful acquaintances.

Listen to Your Children

When your children want to talk, listen carefully to what they have to say. Give them your full attention and try to see any issue that comes up from their perspective.

Talk with your children instead of at them. Making a conversation a "give-and-take" interaction leads to better relationships. Also, find the right time to talk. Some times are better than others. For instance, bedtime is a good time to recap your children's day and talk with them about what's going on in their lives. Dinnertime also provides an opportunity for family members to share routine information, special memories, and family plans with one another. And for the many families that always seem to be on the run taking children to sports and other activities, time spent riding in the car can be used for catching up with each other.

How you talk and listen to your children is important, especially when it comes to preventing or helping them solve problems. Get at their eye level and eliminate distractions. Ask open-ended questions that encourage them to share how they are thinking and feeling. For example, you can ask questions like, *"How did that make you feel?"*; *"What do you think about...?"*; or *"What do you plan to do?"* Asking open-ended questions will obtain more information and keep your conversation from turning into an interrogation.

Help your children feel comfortable when they tell you things by allowing them to take the lead in the conversation. Sit down, keep your arms relaxed, use pleasant and receptive facial expressions, and nod occasionally. The most important thing to do is be quiet! Let your children talk; don't interrupt with advice or ways to fix things. Some parents make the mistake of rushing in and overwhelming their children with advice when they have a problem. Even when your children tell you something that upsets you, try to remain calm and hear them out. Keep your cool, especially when they tell you things that go against your beliefs or that honestly frighten you. You cannot help them come up with solutions to their problems if you don't know the whole story. Remember, their "child" world is usually completely different from our "adult" world. They see things differently because they don't have the experiences adults have had. They need time to talk and figure out how to handle these situations. There will be plenty of time when they've finished talking to work on resolving the issue.

There will be times when your children are vague about a problem they're having with friends, classmates, or what they're hearing and seeing in the media. They won't want to tattle on their friends, and they might be embarrassed to tell you about certain issues (for example, sex or dating). They might be worried they will lose their friends if they tell you about something those peers have said or done, or tried to persuade your children to do. They also may worry about your reaction. At the same time, they may be confused and,

345

deep down inside, really want your help. That's why making them feel comfortable talking to you is very important. By listening calmly, asking brief clarifying questions, and being understanding, you can help your children "open up" when they are having problems.

It's extremely important to praise your children when they do share their thoughts and opinions with you, stand up to negative influences, report a concern, or tell you about a problem. Reinforce their decisions; let them know when they did the right thing. If things didn't work out as well as expected, praise their courage for trying. A few words of support can go a long way toward helping them be more confident in their abilities to arrive at good decisions in the future. For example, you can simply say, *"Thanks for telling me that. It took a lot of courage,"* or *"You should be proud of yourself for standing up to those guys,"* or *"I know it was hard for you to tell me, but now that we know what the problem is, we can deal with it together."*

Monitor, Monitor, Monitor

We can't totally isolate our children from friends, classmates, other peers, or media messages. But we can monitor what they do, who they hang out with, and what they are watching, listening to, and logging in to.

Monitoring means keeping track of and watching over your children, and having them check in and report where they are, who they're with, and what they're doing. It also can involve getting to know their friends and classmates, getting to know those children's parents, and establishing a network where parents can keep in touch about their children's activities.

Some parents can take the idea of monitoring too far. They might want to constantly hover over their children, follow them wherever they go, or try to conduct some kind of undercover surveillance on them. While this might give parents greater peace of mind, it is not a positive or practical approach. Being overprotective and smothering can choke off children's independence, and worse, make them resentful of their parents for what the children see as "spying."

Here's how one parent monitored her four children. She posted this note in a highly visible place on the refrigerator (a spot she knew her children would visit often): "Before you ask me to go anywhere, be prepared to tell me the telephone number where you'll be, how you'll get there and back, if you might be late and why, what you'll be doing, and who you'll be with and the names of their parent(s)." She also made sure the computer was in an open area of the house (not in any of the children's bedrooms), and took steps to block access to harmful websites. None of the children had a TV in his or her room and their TV viewing was limited to channels and programs Mom deemed appropriate. The children's phone plans had minimal data plans, as well.

This parent tried to monitor what her children were doing when they weren't at home, and made every attempt to make sure they were using the computer and their phones properly. Most importantly, this parent consistently delivered consequences for her children's behavior — positive consequences for following the rules and negative consequence for breaking the rules.

Regardless of whether your children are young or old, monitoring their activities keeps you involved and lets them know you care about them and their safety. An additional benefit is that your children will have fewer opportunities to get into trouble because they aren't spending too much unsupervised time with their peers.

Monitoring and checking on your children is one way to alert them to pitfalls, teach and discipline them, and help them solve problems on their own. Monitoring also gives you many more opportunities to "catch them being good," and to use Effective Praise.

Encourage Your Child to Be "Counter-Cultural"

Advertisers, marketers, and other media "persuaders" spend a lot of time and money trying to convince young people they have be cool to fit in, and trying to sell what they claim is necessary to do that. Their message is, "Everyone your age is buying or doing this; don't get left out."

This form of cultural peer pressure is used to sell clothing, shoes, soft drinks, food, toys, computer games, cosmetics, movie tickets, CDs — anything that allows product makers to tap into the gigantic pool of buyers that is the youth market. And why not? Children from age 8 and up are now spending and influencing others to spend more than an estimated $500 billion annually on consumer products.

Such media influence can be harmful when it continually pounds children with the message that there is something wrong with them, or that they don't quite measure up to an impossible standard being set by the marketers. When children start believing that message, their lives can become a never-ending quest to keep up with or surpass their friends, and youth culture in general, in terms of looks, material possessions, and lifestyle. Worse yet, they can begin measuring their worth and the worth of others solely in terms of what they have or don't have.

One way you can prevent this from becoming a problem in your home is to encourage your child to be independent and unique, and not be a slave to every passing fad. Talk with your child about the latest pop-culture craze, "celebrity" spokesperson, or product. What does he or she really think about the messages? Discuss the difference between being a leader and being a follower. Ask how your child and his or her friends can demonstrate their independence from the "herd mentality" marketers are trying to sell. And be a role model when it comes to your own shopping habits by resisting fads, impulse buying, and trying to keep up with the neighbors. Your behavior will have more impact on your children than any lecture you can give.

(For a more detailed look at how you can identify and counter harmful media messages, check out the Boys Town book, *"Who's Raising Your Child? Battling Marketers for Your Child's Heart and Soul,"* by Laura Buddenberg and Kathleen McGee, available from the Boys Town Press®.)

Peer Pressure in Cyberspace

In addition to media messages, another kind of peer pressure has erupted out of the communication age. As texts, emails, instant messaging, chat rooms, social-networking sites, and blogs have become the electronic connections of choice for most children, more and more young people (and adults) have found ways to use and misuse cyberspace to invade people's lives and homes. These online perpetrators include bullies (we refer to them as cyberbullies), sexual predators, sexual con artists, scammers, rumor-spreaders, gossipers, and a variety of other wrongdoers whose aim is to manipulate, intimidate, harass, control, tease, or otherwise use other people for their own pleasure or gain. Even something that seems innocent, like two young people having an online dating relationship, can potentially lead to hurtful behaviors.

In today's technological age, computer users with malice in mind can troll far beyond their physical reach with virtual anonymity as they cruise for potential victims. For your child, this can create uncomfortable, threatening, and even dangerous situations because he or she never knows who's really on the other end of an online conversation. Also, bullying that was once confined to the school day or the playground has now found its way online to threaten and harass some children. Kids can be victimized by rumors, gossip, lies, and intimidation spread through texts and emails, chat rooms, and instant messaging by their peers. Parents not only have to be aware that such problems exist, but also must take action to educate and protect their children.

What can parents do to protect their children in the boundary-free environment of cyberspace where deception is easy, privacy is an illusion, and anonymity is an excuse for an "anything goes" attitude? The starting point is setting boundaries for online behavior, providing consequences when boundaries are broken, and specifically telling your child how and when the computer and phone can be used. Most of these measures apply to just about any situation where someone is misusing the Internet or other programs, and can improve your ability to keep tabs on all of your child's online activities.

Teach Online Etiquette

We recommend that parents teach their children the following four rules about computer and phone use:

- No profanity, threats, mean comments, sexual comments, or inappropriate personal questions and conversations (started either by the child or others).

- Do not give out your name, parent's name, address, phone number, passwords, credit card numbers, and other personal information about yourself or the family.

- If you receive harassing or sexual messages or are the subject of rumors, tell Mom or Dad immediately.

- Be honest. If others are with you while you are online, let the people you're chatting with know you are not alone, and tell them who else is in the room. Don't let anyone pretend to be you.

Children are more likely to remember and follow these rules if you write them down and post them on or near the computer. You can also create a phone and Internet contract, which your child signs as a promise to follow the rules you've set. When your child uses the phone or computer improperly, use Corrective Teaching to remind him or her of the family's rules.

Monitor Computer Use

Computers should be located in common areas like family rooms or dens, not in your children's bedrooms. This makes it easier for you to keep an eye on who is using the computer and how it is being used.

Know your children's passwords and usernames. Let them know you are watching their online activity. (Programs are available that allow you to print out instant messages word for word.) In your house, you have a duty to protect your children. They need to know texting, instant messaging, and Internet use are privileges, and they can be taken away if they are misused. Limit phone data usage plans and set rules on texting.

When children know you can check the websites they visit, read their instant message conversations, or go into their blogs or personal webpages, they are less likely to put themselves in bad situations.

You also can limit your children's screen time. Base the amount of time they can be on the computer on their age and maturity.

You will not be able to catch everything your child sends or receives on a phone or computer. But periodic checks and letting your child know you can and will check is a good way to head off trouble and gain insights into your child's computer behaviors.

Use Consequences

Children love to test boundaries. If you discover your child is misusing his or her phone or computer privileges, take those privileges away for a reasonable amount of time. If your child follows the rules or lets you know of a threat or an inappropriate request or comment from someone who's contacted him or her on the phone or online, give a positive consequence. The idea here is to encourage positive and appropriate use of the phone and computer, and to reinforce the idea your child should tell you about anyone who is sending inappropriate messages to him or her.

Check Buddy Lists

Some instant messaging programs have space for up to 200 names on a buddy list. That's way too many, and your child should only have the names of people he or she can trust and identify for you. If your child doesn't know who someone is, delete the name from the list. Make periodic checks of these lists to make sure your child isn't adding new, unidentifiable "buddies" on the sly.

Take Threats Seriously

Teach your children to contact you immediately if someone online threatens to hurt them or someone else. The same goes for anyone who starts asking personal or sexual questions. If you are not home at the time, your children should stop the online conversation immediately, turn off the computer, and contact you. If they can't reach you, make sure they have a back-up number, such as a relative or the Boys Town National Hotline® at **1-800-448-3000.**

Above all, teach your children that, under no circumstances, should they ever agree to meet or try to meet someone they've met on the Internet without your knowledge of the person and approval.

For more information on peer pressure, bullying (and cyberbullying), youth relationships, and the influence of the media, we recommend the following books from Boys Town:

- *Dating! 10 Helpful Tips for a Successful Relationship* (2013), by Laura Buddenberg and Alesia K. Montgomery

- *Friend Me: 10 Awesome Steps to Fun and Friendship* (2012), by Laura Buddenberg and Alesia K. Montgomery

- *No Room for Bullies* (2005), by José Bolton and Stan Graeve

- *There Are No Simple Rules for Dating My Daughter!* (2006), by Laura Buddenberg and Kathleen McGee

- *Boundaries: A Guide for Teens* (2000), by Val J. Peter and Tom Dowd

- *What's Right for Me? Making Good Choices in Relationships* (1998), by Ron Herron and Val J. Peter

- *Who's in the Mirror? Finding the Real Me* (1998), by Ron Herron and Val J. Peter

- *A Good Friend: How to Make One, How to Be One* (1998), by Ron Herron and Val J. Peter

Summary

Peer pressure, no matter what the source, will always have an influence on your child — sometimes good, sometimes bad. But don't fail to recognize how much influence you have. You can help your children learn to recognize negative peer pressure and teach them what to do about it. Even if you feel your children have already been negatively influenced by peer pressure, it's not too late to start making changes for the better.

In today's world, young people have to learn how to deal with peer pressure from many sources. They will continue to be exposed to personal peer pressure from friends and classmates. There will always be the influence of advertising, marketing, and popular culture in general. And people who misuse the Internet, whether they be your child's own acquaintances, or strangers and even predators, will continue to pose a more sinister and potentially dangerous threat.

As a parent, you face a monumental challenge in teaching your child how to identify, resist, and not be a victim of peer pressure. Like any parenting situation, your success will depend on building a trusting, loving relationship with your child and your ability to use the many parenting tools and skills you have at your disposal.

✌ CHAPTER REVIEW

What are the two main kinds of peer pressure?

Personal peer pressure comes from face-to-face contact with friends, classmates, or other children of the same age. Cultural peer pressure comes from sources like the media and online communication.

How do monitoring, listening, spending time, and solving problems with children help them avoid negative peer pressure?

These relationship-building skills allow parents to influence their children's choices in friends and prepare and teach them how to make good decisions on their own.

Why is it important to use open-ended questions when talking with your children about difficult situations?

Children are more likely to share things with parents and be less defensive. This also allows children to take the lead in conversations.

What parenting skills can you use to help your children make good friends and develop independent decision-making skills?

Preventive Teaching, the **SODAS** problem-solving method, and Effective Praise.

How can parents protect their children when they use the Internet?

Set rules, give consequences to enforce the rules, monitor computer use, follow up on threats or suspicious activity, and check your children's buddy lists.

☆ ACTION PLAN

1. Take some time to answer the following questions:

   - What is the most important thing you learned in this chapter?

   - What do you plan to do differently as a result of what you've learned?

2. At your next Family Meeting, put the topic of peer pressure on the agenda. Invite your children to take the lead in discussing how peer pressure affects them through their personal relationships, at school, in the media, or on the Internet. Ask them what they can do and how you can help them to avoid or resist peer pressure.

Q&A

FOR PARENTS

Q **Do I have the right to insist that my son avoids friends who consistently encourage him to break rules?**

A Yes. Your first priority is your child's safety and well-being. However, you should encourage and teach your son to make good decisions regardless of what his friends think and do. Every day, have him practice using the **SODAS** method with a pretend "friend" issue. This will show you and your child that he's prepared for difficult situations involving his friends and negative peer pressure.

Q **What should I do if my daughter hangs around with friends who are much older than she is?**

A No matter how mature your daughter might seem, it's almost always wise to have her interact with friends within a year or two of her own age. Try getting her involved in various extracurricular activities after school that provide her with an opportunity to be around and make friends with children her own age.

Q **My preteen son thinks I'm overprotective. He says other parents allow their children to do things that I consider inappropriate, like having unsupervised parties, later curfews, and dating. Should I lighten up on my belief that he's too young for these kinds of things?**

A Every family is different. Rules, beliefs, and values will vary from household to household. It's a good idea to listen to your child's point of view without making judgments. But, common sense should always prevail when it comes to allowing your child to face any new challenge. You will want to make sure he is properly prepared to make good decisions, is capable of withstanding peer pressure, and is willing to take responsibility for his behavior without argument on a regular basis before he can earn these kinds of more mature privileges.

Q **How can I keep my child safe from Internet sexual con artists when I'm not very computer savvy?**

A Teach your child the two golden rules about using the Internet safely and responsibly: 1) NEVER give out any identifying information (name, address, phone number, pictures, etc.) to someone; 2) NEVER have a face-to-face meeting with someone you meet online without a parent's knowledge of the person and approval.

Q **I think my daughter may be developing bad habits like gossiping and spreading rumors when she texts, emails, or sends instant messages to her friends. What can I do about this?**

A Children use a different language when they text, email, and instant message each other. Sometimes, it can be hard to figure out exactly what they are saying. If you have concerns and suspicions that your child is engaging in gossip or rumor-spreading, ask her about it. Using the computer is a privilege and misuse should lead to negative consequences. Also, discuss your concerns about this issue at Family Meetings. Express your expectations and set your tolerances regarding this kind of behavior. Let your daughter know you will be monitoring her progress and make a plan to follow up with her at a later date.

Q **Recently, we started getting some really inappropriate emails from someone we don't even know. What can we do about it?**

A First, do not open or respond to the emails. Delete them immediately. Many times, these emails have a virus that can damage your computer or flood it with inappropriate emails and/or "pop ups." Instead, write down the email sender's address and call your Internet service provider. They can help you put up blocks to these kinds of emails and help you figure out the best route to take regarding Internet security and safety.

WRAPPING IT UP

We've given you a lot of information in this book. We hope you will be able to adapt our positive approach and apply all the strategies and parenting skills we've discussed to your relationship with your kids.

One truth should be very clear. Parents don't always have all the answers. After all, children don't come with instruction booklets. Most parents want to find ways to help their children, and by doing so, help themselves. Reading this book and learning new parenting tools shows you have a commitment to becoming a better parent. You want to find answers to questions you can't answer and solve problems you haven't been able to solve. But don't stop here! Continue to learn and grow as a parent.

Because you're doing something new and different, it might take a while before things really start to click. You might get frustrated and your children might question what you're doing and why you're changing how you've parented in the past. They might complain more and even get angry or upset. Don't let this slow you down or discourage you. Move ahead with the confidence that these changes will be best for you and your family in the long run.

Change is always hard in a family, for parents and children. But you don't have to go through these changes alone. Remember, when times get tough and you need a helping hand, Boys Town is always there. Call the Boys Town National Hotline® (**1-800-448-3000**) for help with any family problems. Trained counselors can respond to your questions every day of the week, 24 hours a day, 365 days a year.

As you begin to apply it in your home, you will find the material presented in this book is invaluable and will help you become a better parent.

Good luck in everything you do to become a better parent. Parenting is an ongoing journey and there really is no finish line. The rewards you gain from loving and caring about your kids may come at unexpected times and in unexpected ways. But they will come into focus more clearly as your children grow and develop, and begin to use the new skills you've taught them to make good decisions. When you and your children work together toward positive goals, your whole family wins!

Quick Reference to Parenting Skills

The four main parenting skills are: Effective Praise, Preventive Teaching, Corrective Teaching, and Teaching Self-Control. There are nine steps repeatedly used to create the different skills. These skills and their steps are listed here, along with starter words to help you clearly communicate when you teach your children how to behave appropriately.

Effective Praise

Effective Praise is praising your child for the positive behavior he or she displays.

1. **Show Approval**
   "Wow! Good Job!" (hug, smile)

2. **Describe the Positive Behavior**
   "You said or did..."

3. **Give a Reason**
   "When you do or say... it's more likely... will happen"

4. **Give a Positive Consequence (optional)**
"You earned..."

Preventive Teaching

Preventive Teaching is teaching your child what he or she will need to know for a future situation and practicing it in advance.

1. **Describe the Desired Behavior**
"I want you to say or do..."
2. **Give a Reason**
"When you do or say... it's more likely... will happen"
3. **Practice**
"Let's try this... show me how..."

Corrective Teaching

Corrective Teaching is responding to your child's problem behaviors with teaching and practicing acceptable alternatives.

1. **Stop/Describe the Problem Behavior**
"You said or did..."
2. **Give a Negative Consequence**
"You lost..."
3. **Describe the Desired Behavior**
"I want you to say or do..."
4. **Give a Reason**
"When you do or say... it's more likely... will happen"
5. **Practice**
"Let's try this... show me how..."

Teaching Self-Control

Teaching Self-Control enables parents to calm their children and teach them better ways to respond when they are upset. It also helps parents remain calm when their children refuse to respond to instructions.

Part 1: Calming Down

1. **Describe the Problem Behavior**
   "You said or did..."

2. **Offer Options to Calm Down**
   "I want you to try to calm down by..."

3. **Allow Time to Calm Down**
   "I'll give you time... I'll check on you in a few minutes"

4. **Check for Cooperative Behavior**
   "Could you please....?"

Part 2: Follow-Up Teaching

5. **Describe the Desired Behavior (Stay Calm)**
   "I want you to say or do..."

6. **Give a Reason**
   "When you stay calm... it's more likely... will happen"

7. **Practice (Stay Calm)**
   "Let's try this... show me how..."

8. **Give a Negative Consequence (for not staying calm)**
   "You lost..."

INDEX

A

B

reaching goals using, 129-
144
when to use, 130-131, 143
chore(s), 77-78, 89, 275, 280-
281, 300
adding, 64-70, 71, 167,
171, 200, 262
jar, 67-69
list, 55, 67
small, 68
clear messages, 8, 37-45, 310
action plan, 43
how to give, 39-41
reason for using, 42
commitment, 8, 292
communication, clear, 13, 15,
37-45, 57, 162, 171, 310
computer use,
buddy lists, 352-353, 356
monitoring, 346-348, 351-
352
online etiquette, 350-351
online threats, 353-354, 358
peer pressure, 349-350
confidence, 6, 14, 117, 130,
180, 226, 234, 249, 343,
361
consequences, 8, 12, 26, 35,
42, 47-77, 56-57, 129-130,
178, 181, 287, 302
action plan, 74-75
brevity, 57
changing behavior by
using, 47-75

clear, 57
consistent, 57
contingency, 51-53, 72,
73, 171
definition of, 48
effective, 48-50, 54,
61-64, 72-73, 77-78,
197
following through with,
57-58
frequency, 50, 52-53, 73,
171
group, 58
individual, 58
ineffective, 53-54, 58-59,
182
immediacy, 50, 52-53, 73,
171
importance, 49-50, 52-53,
69, 73, 171
negative, 10, 16, 36,
47-58, 62-76, 126-127,
159, 164, 167-168, 171,
173-174, 179, 182-183,
189, 194, 197, 200,
202, 207-208, 216,
231, 262, 299, 347,
352, 359, 364
pairing with behavior,
61-64, 66
planning ahead, 54-56,
71, 202
positive, 16, 36, 47, 49,
51-62, 69, 71-78, 103-
105, 107, 109, 126-127,

tages, 246-247, 267-268
coming up with, 244-246
tips for identifying, 245-
246
outcomes, natural and logical,
86-87

P

parenting plan
action plan, 302-303
definition of, 292-294,
302
developing, 4, 291-305
how to use, 298-300, 304
importance of, 297-298,
302
single parents and, 305
steps to creating, 302
when to use, 300-301
writing down, 292
patience, 117, 218-219
peer pressure, 4, 113, 300-301,
307-308, 337-359
action plan, 356
cultural, 338-340, 355
cyberspace, 349-351
media, 339-340, 348-349,
354-355
parenting versus, 340-
342, 353
personal, 338-340, 354-
355
Peter, Val J., 354

positive correction, 177, 179,
295
positive teaching, 16-17, 18, 38
definition of, 13
examples of, 14-15
"possibility" words, 86
practice, 15, 34, 36, 87, 95,
112-117, 120-127, 161, 167,
169, 172-175, 179, 180, 191,
196, 215, 217, 249, 296-
297, 364-365
praise, 16, 26, 32, 42, 47, 56,
60, 73, 77, 93-94, 97-110,
109, 117, 127, 136-137, 170,
199, 212, 255, 258, 260,
265, 269, 293, 319, 331,
346, 363
brevity, 102
effective, 94, 97-110, 126,
164, 171, 178, 182,
213, 218, 297, 299,
303, 335, 348, 355,
363-364
general, 98-99
specific, 99
when to use, 99-100, 109-
110
Preventive Teaching, 24, 27,
111, 126-127, 164, 171, 178,
181-182, 187, 207, 212, 259,
264-265, 279, 295-298,
303, 355, 363
action plan, 124-125
definition, 112, 124
examples of, 119-123